MW00331185

PRAISE FOR TC

Read this book, teachers! You need it. You need a space to consider, reflect and recharge. This book will help you do just that. Stay in this fight with us, and let this awesome book be the food you need to keep doing what's best for students right where you are!

— Jayme Rawson

In his book *To the Edge*, Kyle transparency shares the personal and professional stories that led him to where he is today, taking the reader on a journey filled with ups and downs, a journey reminding us that learning to fly requires leaving the safety of the nest. Can that be scary? Absolutely. But consider the view that can only be seen from the air! Let To the Edge encourage you to take those risks, to soar as an educator.

— Brent Coley

What an amazing journey! Only knowing a little of Kyle's story from the time being his coach and teacher in our little town of Alpena, it was great to see the next steps in his quest for excellence. I am always intrigued to know how my former students and athletes turned out and now I know "The rest of the story" as if it was told by the late Paul Harvey about Kyle Anderson. His trials and tribulations are amazing. As he put in the end, the hope that his story will hit home and provide someone with some self-reflection and inspiration is spot on. You cannot help but put yourself in Kyle and Mary's shoes while their life is confronted with many obstacles that every young couple faces when they "try to figure it out". I am not sure that we ever do, but these two will give you a "shotgun" seat ride to their success. Check the coolant level, make sure the AC is working, strap in, and enjoy the ride.

— JASON GRIBBLE

TO THE EDGE

SUCCESSES & FAILURES THROUGH RISK-TAKING

KYLE ANDERSON

EduMatch Publishing

Copyright © 2020 by Kyle Anderson

Published by EduMatch®

PO Box 150324, Alexandria, VA 22315
www.edumatchpublishing.com

All rights reserved. No portion of this book may be reproduced in any form without permission from the publisher, except as permitted by U.S. copyright law. For permissions contact sarah@edumatch.org.

These books are available at special discounts when purchased in quantities of 10 or more for use as premiums, promotions fundraising, and educational use. For inquiries and details, contact the publisher: sarah@edumatch.org.

Cover photo by asoggetti on Unsplash

ISBN: 978-1-970133-64-6

CONTENTS

Foreword   vii

Introduction   xi

1. Life Decisions   1
2. Becoming Battle Born   15
3. Is This Really What I Want in My Life?   33
4. Renewed & Flourishing   45
5. Leadership?   59
6. Changes   71
7. Struggles   85
8. Swimming in the Deep End   99
9. Doing What's Best   111
10. What Are You Waiting For?   123
    Acknowledgments   129
    Notes   133
    Other EduMatch Titles   137

About the Author   157

FOREWORD

I simply cannot imagine being prouder of Kyle and of this book. You NEED to read it. If you're an educator—whether you've been burned out or burnt up, you NEED to read this book. If you're not an educator, but wonder what this job really looks like, or even better, wonder IF you just took a risk, or made a change, or learned a thing, or reached out, or shared a story or an experience or an interaction or... well, you NEED to read this book.

Yes, this book is the story of Kyle. In it, Kyle talks about what shaped him and the decisions he's made, the risks he's taken throughout his life. But it is also my story, your story, OUR story. It is the story of how transformation happens: somewhere in the space between the starting gun and the finish line, we find our *why*, we find our power, our strength, our purpose. We all start out running—but don't always know where we are headed. Sometimes, we don't even know if we are on the right track, right path, right road. We can't run with our heads down—we have to keep them up —and keep our eyes focused forward on the next goal, the next horizon, the next risk worth taking.

Kyle's story and this book will remind even the most battle-worn among us that there is always another breath, another chance, another day. We have to keep running, toward the horizon, right up to the edge, and when it's right—we have to JUMP.

This book came just in time for me; it ran right up alongside me and made me ask myself some vital questions about where I'm going, and what's next on the horizon for me. This is what it will do for you, too.

Kyle's engaging style, his ability to weave a story together, his honesty, humor, and heart will lead you, chapter by chapter, to some questions worth probing in your own life. These questions will help you connect with stories you may need to tell, and will help you plot your course toward your own vital edge, where you'll be able, with Kyle's unique encouragement and support, to JUMP—and go for the things you want —and be proud of every chance you take, regardless of the outcome.

We are here for a purpose. We are here to make this place and ourselves better. But the world can chew us up so thoroughly that we can lose sight of that purpose. Don't spend one more minute, just running for its own sake. Get back on YOUR path, open doors to YOUR future. Take Kyle's work as a meditation, a reflection, and a journey with your new best friend and brother in arms, Kyle.

Trust me. Read the book. Get back on track. Take it to the EDGE. We only have this one life—this one chance to make a difference and to make our lives count. Don't miss out. Don't hold yourself back. Read this book. Take this journey—right to the EDGE.

Kyle continues to be my favorite teaching partner and has inspired me in more ways than he will ever know. Thank you for sharing your journey, Kyle, with me and with all of us. There is no better brother out there.

Jayme P. Rawson is the Achievement Coach at East Career and Technical Academy and serves as the Region II Director for Magnet Schools of America. When she's not helping students with their post-high school plans, she can be found traveling the country, coaching teachers on Project-Based Learning, collaboration, and staying connected to their passion for teaching by finding ways to be creative and take risks with students in the classroom every day. She even makes time to yell either at or with those in the halls of power in the hope that teachers' voices and students' needs always and in all ways come first. She is honored to have been asked to write this fore-word, and hope she did it justice.

INTRODUCTION

 Life is so short

Close to the edge of another backdoor

Life is so sure!

Life will be ready to twist up your world

— To the Edge by Lacuna Coil

The room was dark, save for a handful of lights that revealed a long table decorated with dinnerware, a beautiful centerpiece, and a few candlesticks. It was quiet, the audience unsure of what they were about to see. A voice of baritone broke the silence, asking, "Are you ready?" To whom the audience wasn't sure. Then, from the right of the stage, one by one, ten individuals proceeded to walk toward the table, and one by one, they took their places. One voice, one that identified itself as George Washington, welcomed the others to their table and asked if they would introduce themselves as well. First, it was Harriet Tubman. Next came Albert Einstein. Jackie Robinson joined in, followed by John Lennon. One after another, each individual introduced them-selves, quickly stating their names and their occupations.

A booming voice, claiming to be Al Capone, demanded to know where he was, how he got there, and what he was doing there. George Washington calmly turned to Mr. Capone and informed he and the rest of the group that they had all been brought together through a mysterious time portal that he had discovered to solve an urgent problem: how should the government of the United States solve the skyrocketing costs of healthcare and ensuring that all Americans have access to quality health care? George proceeded to tell the group that he had brought them to his home at Mount Vernon to discuss this issue around his dinner table and hopefully come up with a solution to the problem.

George recognized that it was a problem, but stated that based on his views of government, it wasn't up to the government to provide health care to the general public. John Lennon chimed in, stating that people needed to come together and look out for one another and care for one another. Al Capone had an idea that it could be easily paid for so long as the cops and the government would leave him alone to conduct his business. For the next fifteen minutes, each individual contributed to the conversation, adding their two cents on how they would help solve the problem of healthcare in America, or how they didn't believe that it was a problem. As the dinner wrapped up, the guests agreed that it was a tough problem to solve and that it was going to take more than a dinner conversation to come up with a viable solution.

Clearly, historical figures cannot enter a time portal and come together to talk about current world issues at dinner (although it would be really cool if they could!). But in my classroom, this fantasy would come alive every year as my students' culminating, year-end review/project. The idea was to combine everything they had learned throughout the year about American history and apply it to the current world, answering that age-old question, "Why do we have to learn about history?" A little bit better than a few review questions and vocabulary words, if I do say so myself.

A few years ago, I was given the assignment to read a short book in preparation for a leadership class. The book was small, short, a little bit bigger than a deck of cards, and only about 100 pages. I was able to knock out this reading in about 20 minutes or so. The book was called *Tough Truths: The Ten Leadership Lessons We Don't Talk About*. And even though it was a quick read, one of the lessons that the author, Deirdre Maloney, highlighted really stuck with me: nobody will find you as interesting as you do. Her focus was that a great leader will provide just enough information about themselves to leave the listener wanting more, but the leader's true focus is to learn more about the other side, not spout on forever about their life. And while I truly believe that this is the case in most scenarios, I'm going to completely contradict Maloney's lesson for the next several dozen pages.

My story is not particularly special. My story is not much different from the typical person's: I have had a lot of high marks and a lot of lows, just like the proverbial roller coaster. Over my 38+ years, a lot of the highs and lows can be attributed to the risks I have taken. The idea behind this book is to share some of the moments in my life where a risk has had me soaring like an eagle but others that had me lower than a snake's belly in a wagon rut. But before we dive into that, perhaps I should introduce myself.

My name is Kyle Anderson. You can classify me into several categories. Son of Marshall and Lori. Brother of Brandi and the late Cody (more on this later). Husband of Mary. Father of Elsa and Reed. Uncle to Shelby, Vance, and Lacey. Friend to many.

> The idea behind this book is to share some of the moments in my life where a risk has had me soaring like an eagle but others that had me lower than a snake's belly in a wagon rut.

Comedian, or at least I like to think that I am funny. College graduate, several times over. Educator of 15 years. Athlete. Sports fan. The list can, and does, go on and on.

I was born in a small town in Louisiana called Hammond. I would love to tell you more about it, but frankly, I don't remember any of it. My mom and dad lived in a lot of different places after they were married in 1978 and before my birth in 1981. Louisiana was one of those places. My sister, brother, and I were all born in Louisiana not far from New Orleans, but my parents' home came calling, and we moved to Alpena, Michigan, when the three of us were all still very young. Alpena would be the place that I would call home for the remainder of my childhood, and when people ask me where I am from, Alpena is still, and always will be, my home. This can also explain my love of Michigan, Michigan State, and the Detroit professional teams, especially the Detroit Tigers and Detroit Red Wings.

Alpena was very typical of a small Midwestern town. There wasn't much to do, jobs tended to be of the blue-collar type, and if you needed to go to a mall to get some school shopping done or make a Costco run, you had to drive a couple of hours south to Saginaw or a couple of hours west to Traverse City (the latter happened to be my town's arch-rival, which made trips to "T.C." a little more interesting). Sometimes, we'd go even further south, about 4 hours, to visit some family near Detroit, where "the cities" had way more than my small town had to offer. However, what Alpena lacked in resources was made up by the abundance of places to fish, play some pond hockey, or pickup football and basketball, and was a relatively short drive from some of the most beautiful and historic places in Michigan, namely Mackinac Island and the glory that is the Upper Peninsula.

Growing up, I was the typical Midwestern boy. I played baseball in the spring and basketball in the winter. When I got to junior high, I started playing football. I hunted a little, and I fished a lot. Some of my fondest memories include putting the boat into a small lake or going to the harbor in Alpena, nestled on the shores of Lake Huron, to fish for perch and walleye with my grandpa and my dad. Once winter flexed its muscles for several months at a time, usually starting in November and lasting through April most years, we drilled holes in the ice to catch the fish. I helped out the neighboring farmers during hay season, stacking bales on trailers and loading them into the barn. I enjoyed school, and I did well. I listened to the classic rock that my dad introduced me to and the country that my mom liked until about junior high when country wasn't cool anymore, and I discovered grunge, alternative, punk, and metal that I still enjoy today. I still love classic rock and have come to appreciate classic country and the country music of my youth, but I cannot get into modern country music.

Growing up, I tended to be somewhat shy. I was always bigger than the other kids, sprouting to 5'9" as a 13-year-old 7th grader, before reaching my current height of 6'2" between 8th and 9th grade. And because I loved grunge, I wore flannel shirts and had long blonde hair. Throw into that mix the obnoxious glasses that I wore at the time, and the fact that I was one of the smart kids (and being smart wasn't necessarily cool), I was somebody that was picked on a bit. As a result, while I had friends, I typically kept to myself and didn't say a lot in class.

Sometime around the middle of my freshman year in high school, something clicked with me. I began to come out of my shell. I started to open up more, speak up in class, and my circle of friends started to expand. Sports helped me with that, as did a class that I was invited to take called Natural Helpers. To be selected for this class, your name had to appear on a survey given to students about who they feel comfortable talking with about different things. The class went over strategies on helping others and learning how to open up and communicate with peers and adults. I give a lot of credit to not only my peers that I had in that class but also the teacher, Mr. Poli, in helping me to become more of the extrovert that I am today. And it was because I was able to open up that I became more of the risk-taker that I am today.

This book isn't about glorifying my life or the decisions that I have made. This book is about highlighting the risks that I have taken, the positives and negatives around those risks, and, hopefully, a way to inspire others to take risks and embrace the successes

Sometime around the middle of my freshman year in high school, something clicked with me.

and failures that inevitably will come along with taking risks.

Remember the dinner at George Washington's house where he and his dinner guests discussed the modern healthcare system? That would have never happened had it not been for the hours of planning and taking the risk to provide something different for my students and their learning.

While many of the stories that I am going to tell have a direct impact on me as an educator, there is definitely going to be some personal influence highlighted here as well. So that being said, buckle up, keep your hands inside the car at all times, and get ready for a wild roller coaster ride!

1. LIFE DECISIONS

 Now, young man, what do you want to do with your life?"

— Matt Foley, Motivational Speaker, played by Chris Farley on Saturday Night Live

My heart was thumping. My stomach was in knots. The music was blasting away, almost deafening. Crunching guitars, pounding drums, and low growls were blaring out of the speakers. I reached up, grabbed my shoulder pads and jersey, and slipped them over my head. A quick squirt of water into my mouth and onto my long blonde locks, and I reached for my helmet. Suddenly, the music was gone. A booming voice instructed my teammates and me to "LISTEN UP!" Once the room was silent, Coach told us that he wasn't going to say much because we already knew what we had to do: it was our game day and no words needed to be said to get us up for that. But, we did have a special guest that wanted to say a few words, an alumnus, a Wildcat, who wanted to send us out with some thoughts before we hit the field.

The crowd of coaches parted, and a familiar face emerged in front of my teammates and me. The face belonged to Tom Izzo, head men's basketball coach of Michigan State University, the Spartans. Mr. Izzo stated that he wanted to wish us good luck in our game and to leave it all out on the field. Then the voice went through the roof, and a garbage can was kicked aside. The next few seconds were a blur, but after the tirade, I was ready to run through a wall. The room exploded into screams and cheers, and Coach Izzo sent us out the door and into the tunnel prepared for war.

Such is the life of a college football player. While a typical game day doesn't consist of a famous alum coming into the locker room for a pep talk, getting fired up to join your teammates on the gridiron is typical and win or lose, I always enjoyed myself. But how did I get to this point?

I decided that I wanted to be an educator at a relatively early age. But like most kids, I changed my mind often throughout my childhood. I wanted to be an astronaut. I wanted to be a firefighter. I wanted to be a police officer. And going into high school, I wanted to be a doctor, a surgeon, to be exact. I was so intent on becoming a doctor that when it came time for registering for elective classes, I chose to enroll in Latin, the language in which many European languages has its roots and the roots of scientific and medical terminology. I figured that if I took Latin, that would give me the upper hand when I eventually went off to college to declare a pre-medical major, graduate, then head off to medical school.

Throughout my freshman and sophomore year of high school, I had some wonderful teachers who really sparked my curiosity. Ms. Wojt, my earth science teacher, made the class entertaining. Mr. Meek, my Latin teacher, took a dead language and made it fasci-

I decided that I wanted to be an educator at a relatively early age.

nating through his uncanny ability to tell a story. Mr. Pintar, my US History teacher, was also a master storyteller and created lessons and activities that engaged the mind. You could say that these teachers and many more, in the words of Tisha Richmond, an educator from Oregon and master of gamification in the classroom, made learning in their classrooms magical. Throughout her book, *Make Learning Magical*, she highlights stories of personal connections she has made with students and activities that she has created to make even the most mundane of tasks interesting, and looking back at my time in school, I had several teachers that were Mrs. Richmond. However, it was Mr. Bell that really began to shift my mindset away from becoming a doctor to becoming a teacher.

Mr. Bell was my biology teacher during my sophomore year. At the time that I had him as a teacher, he had been teaching for well over 20 years, perhaps closer to 30 years. The man had thousands of students throughout his career and very easily could have gone through the motions in his remaining time until retirement, but his passion for his craft wouldn't allow him to do such a thing.

Mr. Bell was a quirky man. He was a perfectionist to the point that when he wrote things on the board, such as the date or the topic of the day's lesson, he would use a yardstick to draw a line, then write the message on the line. He even went as far as erasing the line once he was done. Some people may have referred to him as obsessive-compulsive, but I think he just liked things a certain way and had his way of doing things.

Mr. Bell also had this somewhat high-pitched and nasally voice when he addressed the class. It wasn't something that he exhibited if you spoke with him one-on-one; it was only when he addressed the class as a whole. He had these unique mannerisms when he addressed us, such as pausing and looking around for a few seconds before he wanted to make a key point. Sometimes, he would even whisper the main point, and if you couldn't hear him, you had to ask for him to repeat it or just move on with your day without knowing what he said. Luckily, I always sat near the front in his class, so I didn't have that issue so much.

But the thing that I most remember about Mr. Bell was not his passion for biology, his OCD complex with writing on the board or how his desk was organized, or his speaking style. While all of those things are very memorable, the thing I most remember about Mr. Bell was his genuine interest in me and my interests and the interests of my class-mates. Mr. Bell would work his full day teaching classes, just like every other teacher, but I cannot even begin to remember all of the times that I saw him at my football, basketball, and baseball games. I would see him at hockey games. My friends would tell me how he would go to their track meets, plays, concerts, and fundraisers around town. Once I got a job working at a restaurant in Alpena called The 19th Hole, a popular bar and grill, I would see him and his wife there, and he would always say hello and ask me how my shift was going. I also remember he would spark conversations with my classmates and me about shirts that we wore, such as band t-shirts or perhaps most memorable for me, the day I came to school wearing a Detroit Red Wings jersey for the first time and a conversation about how "they have a great chance to win the Cup again." (for the record, I had Mr. Bell during the 1997-1998 school year, a few months after the Red Wings had ended a several decade Stanley Cup drought and won in 1997, only to win it again at the end of that school year).

It is because of Mr. Bell that I decided that I wanted to be a teacher. Namely, I wanted to be a biology teacher. His knowledge and passion for the subject, as well as his relationship building skills, lit a fire underneath me that no other teacher had done

> The thing I most remember about Mr. Bell was his genuine interest in me and my interests and the interests of my classmates.

previously. Now that doesn't mean that I didn't have amazing teachers before that; Mr. Stoll, Ms. Wallis, Mr. Reynolds, Mr. White, Ms. Clute, Mr. Romstadt, and many others made my elementary and junior high school years memorable and enjoyable. But Mr. Bell really took it to the next level, truly convincing me, inadvertently on his part, that my calling in life would be that of an educator. And for the rest of high school, many more teachers would feed fuel into this fire, teachers like Mr. Poli, Ms. Dewitt, Mr. Doubek, Mr. Linton, and Mr. Bennett, the latter two inspiring me not only to become a teacher but to become a coach as well.

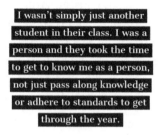

I wasn't simply just another student in their class. I was a person and they took the time to get to know me as a person, not just pass along knowledge or adhere to standards to get through the year.

What was the common denominator amongst each of the names that I mentioned? It was their ability to forge a relationship with students. Clearly, each of these teachers influenced me positively because of the relationships that they built with me and my peers. I wasn't simply just another student in their class. I was a person, and they took the time to get to know me as a person, not just pass along knowledge or adhere to standards to get through the year (although each of these teachers was very good at those as well). And relationships may be the most important factor in what it takes to be an effective teacher. We will explore this idea further in Chapter 3.

NOW THERE ARE multiple paths to achieving your goal, regardless of what career path you take. Some people graduate high school and enroll in a traditional four-year college program. Others take care of the prerequisite credits through a community college program before moving on to a four-year school. Others enlist in one of the branches of the military, complete some credits while in the service, then finish their degree after their military career has concluded. Then there are those that work a job for a few years and go back to school much later on. I was no different than the rest of my friends and classmates; I had decisions to make regarding my future, with advice, both welcomed and unsolicited, coming from multiple directions.

So, I think that in order to fully understand my decision-making process, you need to understand a little bit about my family history. Outside of a couple of my older cousins, people in my family did not go to college. I came from a military family. My father spent a couple of years in the Army in the late 1970s. My maternal grandfather served in the Army during World War II, as did his brothers, my great uncles. My paternal grandfather also spent time in the Army. My Uncle Jim, while not family by blood, but by marriage, served in the Army in Vietnam. My mother's three brothers, Rick, Mike, and David, all served in the Navy, with my Uncle Rick retiring from the Navy, Uncle Mike receiving a medical discharge after 11 years, and Uncle David serving four years. Several cousins from both sides of my family enlisted in the Army, Navy, Marines, Air Force, and Coast Guard. So it did not come as a surprise during my junior year of high school that many family members asked me if I was going to enlist in one of the branches of the military. Even without prodding from my family, the thought had crossed my mind, with my thoughts leaning mostly toward the Navy.

I even got advice from one of my father's colleagues from work. This particular man had attended the United States Naval Academy in Annapolis, Maryland. He had earned a world-class education in four years at the Academy, then served four years as a Naval officer before discharging and making a living as a civilian. He told me that based on my academic successes and my interest in the Navy, I would be a great candidate to attend the Academy, earn my degree, serve the requisite time in the active-duty Navy after the Academy as an officer, then still have practically my entire life ahead of me as a civilian to do whatever I wanted. As a 17-year-old kid, the thought of attending the Naval Academy and serving as an officer in charge of enlisted men and women was intriguing, yet frightening at the same time. But I filed it in my mind as an option for my future.

There was also the option to attend community college. My hometown of Alpena has Alpena Community College, a great option for those that want to stay closer to home before going on to a four-year school. ACC, at the time that I was finishing up high school, was an option for those that wanted to become a nurse through its registered nurse program, a teacher through its partnership with Michigan four-year colleges, or a concrete technologist by completing its concrete technology program, which to this day is the only program of its kind in the world.

I didn't give much thought to attending ACC. Part of me was ready to leave my hometown to experience something else; part of me didn't want to simply continue on to "13th and 14th grade," a common expression among my peers in reference to how staying at home to go to community college would be an extension of high school. Something else was drawing me to pull me away from home.

As I HAVE PREVIOUSLY MENTIONED, athletics were a big part of my life. I started playing tee-ball, then baseball when I was five years old, then basketball when I was nine. Football and hockey were always things that I enjoyed, but my town didn't have a youth football program until junior high, and hockey was expensive, something that my family could not afford. When I started seventh grade, I began playing football for the Alpena Raiders. Our team traveled to play teams from small towns throughout Northern Michigan, with each team named after a professional team like the Sault Ste. Marie Giants, the St. Ignace Jets, the Alcona Packers, the Tawas Lions, the Onaway Falcons, and the Cheboygan Rams. The helmets and jerseys replicated the professional teams. Even the league itself was called the NFL, the Northern Football League. Once I started playing football, I knew I had found a sport that I was going to focus my energies upon.

The following year, I planned to play for the Raiders again, but the team folded, leaving me to find another football team. The Tri-County Falcons were a brand new team in the next town over, Hillman. With my experience playing for the Raiders and the Falcons, I knew going into high school that football was my favorite. I would continue to play baseball and basketball, playing four years of baseball in high school and three years of basketball, earning three letters combined, but football was my tunnel vision. Workouts were geared toward getting bigger and stronger. In fact, because I was no longer working my muscles for effective throwing and batting, my skills in baseball deteriorated. And because I was always so much bigger than kids my age on the basketball court, I never truly learned how to shoot long-range shots and ball handle because I could simply post up and score, rebound, and block shots, so once my peers began to catch up to me, I was left behind in basketball as well.

Toward the end of my junior year, I began to receive interest from a small number of colleges regarding my academic successes and my abilities on the football field. Big-name schools weren't necessarily calling, as I was very much undersized for my position as an offensive lineman in comparison to what Division I schools typically recruit for that position. However, I began to get some interest from a few Division II and Division III schools. But even though the schools were calling with interest, they weren't offering much in terms of money to pay for school, something that was certainly on the front burner in my decision to either go to school, enlist in the Navy, or apply for acceptance into the Naval Academy. My grades and test scores were going to pay for some of it, but one school, in particular, that was interested in me offered about $5,000 in academic scholarship, no athletic scholarship, and cost over $20,000 a year for tuition, fees, room, and board. That being said, I didn't give that school much thought at all.

Between my junior and senior year, my parents took me on some official visits to a couple of schools, Northern Michigan University and Michigan Technological University. I had also visited Central Michigan University when I attended their football camp that summer and got to see the campus and facilities. During this time, I had also been talking to the Navy recruiter and was still contemplating the process of applying to the Naval Academy. While each choice of school, enlistment in the Navy, or the Academy had its advantages, I also weighed out the risks of each decision.

The Navy had an extensive list of options for jobs; I was especially interested in cooking, and the Navy would train me in the culinary arts. The Navy would allow me to see different parts of the world, from basic training in Chicago to any number of stations where I would be sent upon completing basic training. The Navy also offered the allure of the GI Bill, earning money to pay for school after leaving the military. But then there were the risks. What if I didn't like the military lifestyle? The Navy isn't like a job or a school where if I didn't like it, I could quit and try something else. Once you have committed, you have committed until you fulfill your enlistment. What if I didn't like my post in which I was assigned? Again, I wouldn't be able to simply pack up and move to another post on a whim. But my thought at the time was that if I enlisted and didn't like it, it was only a four-year commitment, and then I could move on with my life.

While each choice of school, enlistment in the Navy, or the Academy had its advantages, I was also weighing out the risks of each decision.

Many of the same risks were associated with the Naval Academy route. But unlike enlisting in the Navy, there was a much longer commitment. Upon completing the four-year academy, newly commissioned office graduates of the Academy are committed to several years of active duty service after graduation. And unlike a regular college, you cannot back out of a service academy appointment, at least not very easily. And to top it off, if you do get out of your commitment, you will be forced to pay the government back the thousands upon thousands of dollars that they committed to your training and education. So the risk of acceptance and enrollment in the Naval Academy was similar to enlistment, but a much stronger and longer commitment. But in the back of my mind, I also reminded myself that I could go just about anywhere with a Naval Academy education and service to my country once I decided to leave the Navy.

Then came the comparisons of the various schools that I visited. Did they have the programs that I wanted (if I wasn't going to the Navy, I wanted to become a biology teacher)? Would I have the chance to play football? Was it something that my family and I would be able to afford? I began to analyze each of the options. Northern Michigan and Central Michigan had both been founded as teaching colleges back in the late 1800s and were still well known for their teaching credential programs. Michigan Tech, on the other hand, did not have a teaching specific program but instead had a biology program that I could complete, but I would have to get my teaching credentials elsewhere upon completion. When I visited Northern Michigan and Michigan Tech, I also met with their football coaches, and while nothing was promised, the door was opened to continue a conversation about playing at a later time. Central Michigan was most likely out of my league, as I was undersized for Division I football. And lastly, each school was within a couple of thousand dollars a year of each other; I qualified for the most academic scholarship with Central Michigan, but they were also the most expensive of the three schools.

So now came the whole process of deciding what to do: apply to schools and narrow it down to one; apply to the Naval Academy; or enlist in the Navy, heading to basic training a few weeks after gradua-tion? I submitted applications to Northern Michigan University, Michigan Technological University, and Central Michigan University. I also enrolled in a dual-enrollment introductory to education course offered through Alpena Community College that I would complete during the spring semester of my senior year of high school where I would take high school classes part-time while attending the class twice a week at the college while earning both high school and college credit. I began the process of applying to the Naval Academy, stopping short of requesting a United States Senator recommendation until more developments began to emerge. I also spoke to the Navy recruiter again, filling him in on the options on the table and informing him that I would be in touch. All options were certainly on the table, but my decision would be made in early November, shortly after my senior season of football ended.

A student aide came to my precalculus class with an envelope. The envelope was addressed to me, care of Alpena High School, with a return address of the football office at Northern Michigan University. Inside was a simple, handwritten note that stated, "Dear Kyle, I would like to talk to you more about Northern. Please contact me ASAP. Sincerely, Eric Holm, Head Football Coach". My teacher let me leave class to go to the counselor's office to make a phone call. My conversation with Coach Holm was quick, but essentially, he informed me that he had received video of a few of my games and a recruiter had been at a couple of my games, and he wanted me to come on an official visit to Northern Michigan University while offering me a spot on the football team for the 2000 season! From that point forward, I knew what I was going to do; I called my mom at home and my dad at work and told them that I was going to go to NMU, study biology education, and play football for the Wildcats!

Now, this story is probably not much different than a lot of people in the latter stages of their high school education. It's not so much my experience, but the risks involved and how much different life would be at this point had I made other decisions. Three key aspects of my life come to mind when I think about this decision in hindsight nearly 20 years later.

First, I would have never met my best friend, my brother, my family that I never knew I had, Brandon Genwright. Brandon is a man that I met at orientation in the weeks before starting college. We both were going to be playing football, and we hit it off at orientation, deciding at the end of the two days that we should be roommates. It could have been a train wreck, but luckily, we both clicked right away. We lived together for four years, sharing everything about ourselves with each other, taking care of each other when we were sick or down, and stood up for one another in all sorts of situations, from our weddings to one night at a bar when a group of tough guys was trying to start stuff with us. To this day, I cannot recall any time where we have had an argument or were mad at one another.

Brandon has certainly made my life better, and I am so very thankful that he is still in my life.

Second, I would have never met my loving wife, Mary, had it not been for my decision to go to Northern Michigan. At the end of my fourth year of college, I had decided to focus on finishing school and left the football team after a terrible injury to my right acromioclavicular joint, the joint that connects the scapula (shoulder blade) to the clavicle (collar bone). I had a grade three separation of the joint just before the first game of the 2003 season and never really was able to get it back into game shape. I decided that it wasn't worth the time and effort to rehabilitate my shoulder for one more year of school, especially since I wasn't receiving much for a football scholarship, and I was only about seven credits short of starting student teaching.

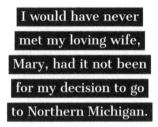

So one night in August 2004, a night that in previous years I would have had to have been in bed to be up the next morning for early practice, I went out with a buddy to see some friends and have a drink. A friend I hadn't seen in a long time happened to be at the bar and introduced me to this beautiful brunette that happened to be at the same Korn and Linkin Park show that I had been at the week prior. We talked for hours, and I asked her if she'd like to have lunch the next day. The rest is history, as we have now been married for 11 years, together for 15, and have two wonderful children together.

Lastly, deciding to leave home at 18, attend college, and play football at a school hundreds of miles away eventually inspired me to take other risks. The risk of changing my major from biology to social studies after my first semester of school. The risk of realizing that my education was more important than football. The risk of moving across the country after graduating from college with a girlfriend of about 10 months, and so much more. We will explore these risks in greater detail in the next chapter!

Often times, risk doesn't have immediate consequences, either positive or negative. It may take several days, weeks, months, even years for you to realize the effects of a risk you have taken. And ultimately, it's these risks that make you a better educator and

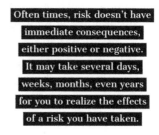

human being. Agonizing over a potential life-changing risk creates learning opportunities. You must weigh out the costs and benefits of any decision you make. To make an informed decision, you must put in the time to learn about the costs and benefits of any decision you make. Sometimes, you will make the right decision and sometimes you won't, and regardless if you believe the risk was worth it or not, one will learn from the decision.

And these risks would have never happened had it not been for the genuine, caring relationships that I had with teachers like Mr. Bell. Brent Coley, in his book *Stories of EduInfluence*, highlights the importance of these relationships and how relationships made an impact on not just his students, especially a young man that struggled academically and behaviorally, but how he became a better educator as a result of realizing relationships were more important than content and classroom management. While I did not struggle in the classroom or misbehave regularly, I attribute my successes and my willingness to take risks to Mr. Bell and a host of others.

Think about a time in your life where you took a risk and didn't realize the impact of your decision until much later. Consider the following questions while pondering this time in your life:

- What major life decision(s) were you considering? What options were on the table surrounding this situation?

- At the time of the decision, did you believe that you made the right one? Why or why not?
- Looking back now, would you have done anything differently? How would your life be different at this point had you taken a different risk?
- What impact has this decision had on you as an educator? Has it had a positive impact? A negative impact? Why do you believe this?

Share your story and your thoughts on Twitter using #ToTheEdgeEDU!

2. BECOMING BATTLE BORN

Hey baby, let's go to Vegas, bet on love, and let
it ride!

— *Let's Go to Vegas* by Faith Hill

The sound of the air conditioner was constant. Even though the apartment was small, the sound coming through the vents seemed to echo, making it even louder. But it was well over 100 degrees outside, even though the sun had been down for a few hours, so the sound of the unit wasn't going away anytime soon. The living room consisted of a recliner that my parents had given me, and nothing more. The bedroom, not much more...just a mattress on the floor. A quick glass of water and I said goodnight to my mother and my girlfriend, Mary. They would sleep on the mattress, and I would take the recliner. I knew that I wasn't going to sleep very well, but tomorrow was going to be a big day, and I needed to get as much rest as possible.

The sun burned through the patio door a few hours later. I decided that there wasn't any use trying to go back to sleep, so I grabbed the keys to the moving truck and padlock on the door of the truck and headed out to the parking lot to start bringing in what I could. After driving for days and getting into the city late the previous day, the only thing that we wanted to do is grab a quick dinner and bring in the recliner and mattress, just enough so that we could get some sleep. But now, it was time to bring in the rest, or at least what we could until help could arrive to get the big stuff like the couch. This was our new home, and it was time to start making it look like home.

As I have previously mentioned, I was born in Louisiana, but do not have a recollection of my time there. In fact, the only true connection that I have to the state is my birth certificate that reads "State of Louisiana" at the top. Because I was so young when my family and I left for Michigan, the only place I really knew from the time that I was about 4 years old until college was Michigan. Winters were LONG! Summers were short, and the weather fluctuated almost by the minute. It would be sunny and 90 one minute, the next it could be 60 and pouring rain with thunder and lightning.

The small town is also all that I knew, save for a few trips to Detroit, Chicago, and my first plane trip in high school to Reno (then the drive from Reno to Las Vegas with my family over the approximate span of a week). Growing up, Alpena seemed big, especially when we got a Walmart when I was 14. According to the United States Census Bureau (2019), the population of Alpena County in 2000, the year that I graduated high school, was 31,314. The City of Alpena was about one-third of that total. And because I lived out in the country, not in the "city," neighbors were few and far between.

So what convinced me, a Midwestern boy growing up in the farm country near a small town to pull up stakes and move to the booming metropolis of Las Vegas? My town was about 10,000 people; Las Vegas has a metropolitan population of nearly 2 million. My home saw six months of winter a year, and Las Vegas was six months of excruciating summer heat. My town had a river, lake, or pond every few miles; Las Vegas has no lakes or rivers beside Lake Mead (remember, I loved to fish and play pond hockey). Let's go back for a quick sojourn into college and my experiences as an undergraduate.

Northern Michigan University is located in Marquette, Michigan, a town about twice the size of my hometown of Alpena. However, that still only makes the town's population about 20,000. Marquette County was also about double the size of Alpena County, with a few more towns than Alpena County, towns like Negaunee, Ishpeming, and Gwinn. The focal point of Marquette was the university, with about 8,000 students enrolled when I started in the fall of 2000. It wasn't the big city, but it was bigger than what I had known, and more importantly, it was something different; I was ready to leave the proverbial nest and stretch my wings.

MARQUETTE AND NORTHERN MICHIGAN UNIVERSITY had a lot to offer a 19-year-old student like myself. There was a variety of classes, the outdoor activities in and around town like hiking, fishing, skiing, and much more. There was also the dorm life, which was not the nightmare for me that it is for so many people that leave home to go to college. At the time, Northern Michigan University assigned two students to a room. Those two students shared a common bathroom with two other students. While some students stuck with the traditional two-person per room living arrangement, some went with the super suite, choosing to put all of the beds in one room and create a social area in the second room. My roommate, Brandon, and I had a unique living arrangement when staying in the dorms.

When we met at orientation, we signed paperwork to be roommates and submitted it to the university. However, the housing department did not get the memo and assigned us to random people. A couple of phone calls later, we were able to straighten out the confusion, but the only room available was a private suite that would only be the one room and bathroom, meaning we did not have to share the bathroom with two other people. Immediately, the question that begged to be asked was, "How much extra is this going to cost in room and board?" Surprisingly, it was only an extra $50 per semester! We jumped all over that proposal and moved into Room 165 of Gant Hall on Northern Michigan's campus shortly after reporting for football camp.

Sadly, Gant Hall is no longer standing, as it was demolished to build new dorms. I will always have fond memories of living in that residence hall, the relatively decent food from the cafeteria in the quad, the mini kitchen Brandon and I set up in our room with a mini-fridge, microwave, toaster, coffee maker, George Foreman grill, and our personal favorite, our electric water pot for making top ramen and when we were sick, our makeshift humidifier!

Brandon and I really grew as friends, as brothers, and as men living in that dorm room.

Brandon and I really grew as friends, as brothers, and as men living in that dorm room. It was there, about 3 weeks after moving in, that Brandon found out that he was going to be a father, a "little" boy named Brandon as well, whom I affectionately call my nephew, and he calls me Uncle Kyle. It was there that we learned to care for one another because nobody else was there to do it for us, like the time Brandon came down with strep throat, which I contracted after nursing him back to health. It was there we both agonized over final exams, relationships with women, and the pain and suffering of the grueling football season, then the even more grueling offseason training program. Brandon was also there when my father called me to tell me that my grandmother had passed away. I cannot thank him enough for his support during the hours after that call of helping me contact my professors and coaches to let them know I would be going home for a few days and helping me pack for the four-hour drive home and the week I would spend with my family. We were nearly inseparable, and it was a no brainer that we would move on from the dorms and get an apartment together after our second year.

Our time together in the apartment we rented was very similar, except now we had to be even more responsible. No longer could we rely on the cafeteria in the quad (not that we didn't have underclassmen on the football team occasionally take us there for dinner, which nowadays may be considered hazing, but even then, it was never something Brandon and I forced our teammates to do, they always had a choice). We had to cook for ourselves, which luckily both of us could do fairly well. In fact, after football ended in the fall of 2002, Brandon put in a good word for me with a friend that worked at Applebee's and got me a job there as a cook, a job that I held onto for the remainder of college.

Things did start to shift in our relationship during our fourth year together, but not in a negative way, just directions that young men start to take once the light begins to be visible at the end of the tunnel. In the fall of 2003, I suffered what would become a career-ending injury to my acromioclavicular, or AC, joint in my right shoulder. It was a grade three sprain, the worst kind of sprain. I distinctly remember how it happened: it was during our first team scrimmage before the season started, a time when most of my teammates and I were fighting for a starting position. I was on the kickoff receiving team as part of the second wedge, a group of four players that the returner would get behind to advance the ball as far upfield as possible or even spring loose for a touchdown. One of my teammates came barreling down at full speed as what I would eventually refer to as in my coaching career as the "tank buster," the man whose sole job is to break up the wedge. I saw him coming and lowered my shoulder, making direct contact with his shoulder. It was a thunderous hit, and we both hit the ground, hard. I immediately knew something was wrong, but this was not the time to see the trainer; this was the time to earn my playing time.

My teammate was also down; I would eventually learn that he suffered from a concussion on the play, and he missed a few days. Me, trying to tough things out, I lined up at my tight end spot off and on for the next 45 minutes. The pain in my shoulder was excruciating, but I kept trotting out there. Eventually, the pain was so intense that I could not get into a three-point stance, let alone use my arm to block or attempt to catch a pass. I reluctantly headed over to the trainer to have them take a look.

I could barely get my shoulder pads off as the pain was shooting through the right side of my body. The student trainer looked at it but thought that I just had a "stinger." Even the head athletic trainer didn't fully understand what was going on and thought that it was something minor. After the scrimmage was over a couple of hours later and the pain becoming worse, even through the bag of ice, I told the trainer that I thought I needed to be checked further, so he arranged to have me taken to the local hospital in Marquette for further evaluation.

I sat in a dark examination "room" for almost an hour. I was alone, I was cold, and my shoulder and arm were pulsing with pain. Finally, a doctor came in and asked me the routine questions of, "How did this happen," "Where does it hurt the most," and "Have you ever done this before?" Upon examining my shoulder, he immediately ruled out a separated shoulder with a resounding, "This is a problem!" I asked him what he thought, and he explained to me in a lot of technical medical jargon the problem as he laid his middle finger between my AC joint. He then informed me that he would give me a sling, some painkillers, and a note that prevented me from any football activities for the next month. Over the next couple of days, I learned two things. One, I hate prescription narcotics. They did nothing for the pain, and they only made me dizzy and nauseous. (I haven't taken anything like that since because of that feeling and the fear of opioid addiction.) Second, my football career was most likely over.

I went through weeks of rehab to get my shoulder back to normal. However, every time it seemed that it was about ready, I would have another setback, and it would lead to several more days of rehab. By the time I finally got my shoulder back to where I could participate in full practices again, I was at the bottom of the depth chart, and the season was nearly over. Without telling anybody, not even my parents, I decided that I would be hanging it up after the last game of the year, even though I had one more year of eligibility left. I knew I had no shot at going pro, the rehab on my shoulder was tedious, I wasn't getting a lot of scholarship money for football, and I was getting close to my student teaching and finishing up my degree. With a heavy heart on the Monday following our last game, I walked into my coach's office and told him that I would not be returning. He thanked me for my hard work and told me that if I changed my mind, I always had a spot on the team. He even offered to bring me on as a student coach, much like a graduate assistant, but I politely declined, feeling that it would be too strange to coach my teammates when I could still be playing with them.

In the meantime, Brandon was lighting up the football field. He was starting at linebacker, recording dozens of tackles a season, returning an interception for a long touchdown at one point, and receiving honors from the team and the conference.

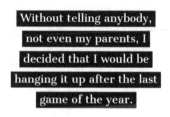

Without telling anybody, not even my parents, I decided that I would be hanging it up after the last game of the year.

After the 2003 season, Brandon's eligibility was up, I was no longer playing, and we both began to focus on our studies. That's when the professional tryout calls started to come for Brandon.

Brandon and I decided that we really needed to look to the following year and the possibility of him living elsewhere while I finished school. I began to look for a new place to live with some friends knowing that Brandon leaving was a real possibility. A group of friends and I signed a lease on a house and began to prepare for our last year of college when Brandon hurt himself in a college all-star game. His shot at a professional tryout was postponed and he was not going anywhere, but I had also already signed a lease. We were both devastated for multiple reasons, but we both decided that things happened for a reason and that we needed to continue our plans: I would be finishing up school and moving in with our friends, and he would stay in our apartment and bring on a new roommate while he finished school.

AS THE FALL semester of 2004 was approaching, it was strange not to be on the field. It was the first time in 10 years that football did not occupy my fall. It freed me up to work a little more to save up for the winter semester when I would be student teaching and allowed me to go out with friends a little more often. It was because of this extra time that my life was changed forever on a Thursday night before the fall semester started.

It was August 12. I had worked an afternoon shift at Applebee's and had gone home to get cleaned up to meet a friend for a drink or two. The original plan was to go to a smaller bar, play some pool, and catch up some. However, when I picked up my friend, he said he wanted to go to another place, one that was a lot louder, more of a dance club type bar—a place that I despised as I was, and still am not, a dancer, nor interested in paying covers and inflated prices for drinks. I grudgingly agreed, telling him he owed me one.

When I entered, it was just as I expected: super-loud, super-dark, and impossible to get to the bar because of how crowded it was. But on my way to the bar, I ran into my friend, Amy. Amy had graduated in the spring and had a fulltime job, and I hadn't seen her in months. We spent a few moments catching up, and knowing I love music, Amy asked if I had been to any concerts. I told her that I had gone to Detroit the previous week to see Linkin Park, Korn, Less Than Jake, and Snoop Dogg. She responded with, "I think my coworker was at that show, let me go get her, I'll introduce you!"

I had been single for several months, wasn't necessarily looking, and certainly wasn't expecting to meet anybody that night. But when Amy brought this woman over, I was awestruck. Mary was gorgeous, she liked the same music as me, and we spent the rest of the night talking and getting to know one another, ending the night with an exchange of phone numbers.

The next day, I broke the cardinal rule: I called her.

The next day, I broke the cardinal rule: I called her. You're supposed to wait a couple of days, or at least back then, but I couldn't wait. I asked if she had time to go have lunch with me before I had to go to work. I met her at a place called the New York Deli, where I had a triple-stacked pastrami and corned beef, and she had a dessert (another reason she was so great, she went straight to dessert!). From that point forward, we were together every moment that we could be. I had my class schedule and work at Applebee's. She had her class schedule and worked at a local hotel, but whenever we had time off from those, we were together and quickly developed a relationship that I thought I had experienced before, but I knew immediately was something much deeper.

Months went on, and I got closer to finishing up school. I was student teaching at a small school about 30 miles from Marquette, working with a high school social studies teacher. The days were busy and weekends even busier, as I was pulling in as many hours as I could at Applebee's to make ends meet. On top of that, I was trying to see Mary as much as I could, and we were starting to get very serious. We had a tradition of seeing a movie every Friday night after we got out of work around midnight, something that I remember looking forward to every week. And through all of this, we began to talk about our future, a future that was beginning to look more and more like a shared future, and a future that was looking to be something drastically different from what we both knew.

THE ECONOMY of Michigan in the early 2000s wasn't the strongest. As a state in the old industrial Rust Belt, Michigan was struggling with the post-industrial economy. Auto plants and factories that had built cities like Detroit, Flint, and Saginaw were suffering, but it wasn't just the blue-collar economy that was tough. All aspects of the job market were slim pickings, including education. The running joke in many schools was that one had to wait for a retirement, then fight off the hundreds of applicants to get a teaching job, and once you were in, you didn't give it up; you stayed there for the next 30 years and retired yourself. Needless to say, the job market for a high school social studies or physical education teacher was mostly non-existent, so unless I wanted to continue working at Applebee's for a while until jobs opened up, I knew that I was going to be leaving Michigan to pursue my career. And as for Mary, she knew that she was going to need to go to graduate school to continue her education before she could find work in her field as a speech-language pathologist, but she also knew that she could also find a well-paying position in a hotel just about anywhere, given her experience with her hotel job throughout college.

As our last semester of undergrad moved along, I began to look for teaching positions. I was not picky, I was looking just about everywhere. I looked at districts throughout Michigan without much luck. I applied for a position outside of Wichita, Kansas, and received a letter thanking me for applying, but never received further word. I looked at some openings near Duluth, Minnesota, but never pursued them because Duluth was even colder than Marquette, and I was sure that I didn't want to go somewhere colder. I received information on districts in Alaska and Bakersfield, California, but after a bit of research, I decided that Alaska was too far away, and Bakersfield did not sound appealing to the 23-year-old me. But when one of the former assistant managers that I worked with at Applebee's came back for a visit, she told me about a little city in which she was working called Las Vegas.

I had been to Las Vegas before. When I was a junior in high school, my spring break vacation with my family consisted of my first ever flight from Saginaw, Michigan, to Reno, Nevada. Over a week, I got to see Reno, Lake Tahoe, and various places in Northern California before we drove south along the US-395 corridor of California to I-40, eventually to Flagstaff, Arizona and a visit to the Grand Canyon. After a night in Williams, Arizona, we went to Las Vegas for a few days with stops at the Hoover Dam and the various tourist traps along the Las Vegas Strip.

The following year, my mother, father, brother, and I essentially repeated the trip (my sister went to Cancun with one of my aunts instead). Instead of the Grand Canyon, this time we drove through Death Valley on our way from Reno to Las Vegas. And because we had been there the previous year, my brother and I skipped a lot of the stuff we had already done and instead tried to find other fun things to do, as much as an 18-year-old and a 15-year-old could do on the Las Vegas Strip. We were able to score some tickets to see Incubus at the House of Blues Las Vegas, a concert that, while nearly 20 years ago, one that I still consider one of the best I have ever been to. The show was shortly after their album Make Yourself was released, which really put the band on the radar for several years; their setlist consisted of a lot of the songs that would become hits from Make Yourself and a mixture of tunes from S.C.I.E.N.C.E. and Fungus Amongus.

I went to Las Vegas a third time in 2004 with my buddy, John VanDusen. He had been trying to convince me for months that we should do something fun for spring break, but I wasn't sure if I could afford anything and frankly, brushed off the idea. However, he found a flight and three nights on the Strip for around $200 about two weeks before our spring break (try finding that kind of a deal to go anywhere now!). I was convinced; John and I got time off of work, scraped up the money to buy flights, reserve a hotel room, and a bit of spending money, and had a really fun spring break, one that was much different than my previous Las Vegas trips when I was under 21 and could not enjoy all that Las Vegas had to offer on those trips.

When my old assistant manager came back, she filled me in on the situation with the school district in Las Vegas and how they had a catastrophic shortage of teachers because the city was growing so quickly. The Clark County School District was hiring several thousand teachers a year, the weather was amazing, and Las Vegas and the surrounding area had tons of great things to do, and was only a few hours' drive from all sorts of places like the Grand Canyon, San Diego, Disneyland, and so much more. I was certainly intrigued, but the decision to go somewhere wasn't just mine. I had to talk to Mary about it as well.

SPRING BREAK for our last year of college was quickly approaching. My spring break would consist of student teaching, as my school's break was not the same as the university's, so I knew I wasn't going anywhere. However, Mary would have a week off from school. I suggested to her that she go to Las Vegas to check it out and see how she liked it, considering that she had never been there before. So Mary and her sister, much like my friend John and I the year prior, scraped together enough money for a flight, a hotel, and some spending money and went to Las Vegas for a few days. Upon her return, Mary told me that she could see herself living and working there, so it was decided: we were going to move to Las Vegas.

Any money that we were pulling in now went straight to our savings accounts to save for the cross-country move. I began to complete the job application process for the Clark County School District, some of which I had to wait on until I graduated at the beginning of May. We began to look for apartments in Las Vegas, a task that was much harder to do online in 2005 than it is today. We didn't look at neighborhoods and their reputations, we looked at what was cheap. We knew we weren't going to be able to afford to go out to Las Vegas to look for a place in person, so we had to rely on the pictures online and the word of the landlord when we made phone calls. So the excitement of finishing up school and becoming a college graduate was doubled with our upcoming move to Nevada, but it wasn't all business; we wanted to reward ourselves for all of the years of hard work that got us to graduation.

Neither Mary nor I had ever been to New York City. A quick search online found plane tickets that would get the two of us there a few days after graduation for under $300. A phone call to some family of mine that lived in New Jersey about 20 minutes from Manhattan, and we had a place to stay. Money that we had both been saving from donating plasma (remember, we were poor college kids, we made money however we could) was our spending money. For a week, we got to see the Statue of Liberty, the top of the Empire State Building, Times Square, Wall Street, the World Trade Center Site (cleanup was still the main focus, as September 11th had only been about three and a half years prior) and eat some of the most amazing food in the world. We got to visit my aunt and uncle and cousins that I hadn't seen in years, Mary got to see one of her cousins that lived in Manhattan, and we got to go to Atlantic City for a day trip with my aunt and uncle to see another cousin that was stationed there in the Coast Guard. Upon returning to Michigan, a quick trip to see some family and take in a Detroit Tigers game, then it was back to Marquette to work for a couple of more months, save as much as we could, then pack up our lives and move over 2,000 miles across the country to start our lives as college graduates.

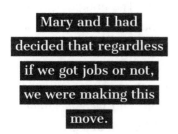

Mary and I had decided that regardless if we got jobs or not, we were making this move. Shortly after returning from our trip to New York, I interviewed by phone with the Clark County School District and submitted the required paperwork to be entered into their hiring pool. It was explained to me that once I was accepted into the pool, my name and profile would be available to principals that needed to fill positions and that I should be receiving some phone calls from prospective employers. In the meantime, Mary applied for various positions in the hotels on the Strip. We were both convinced that the job market would be good to us, so neither of us was worried about getting a job—it was a matter of when, not if.

A few days after my phone interview with the district, I received a phone call from the principal of an online high school. The concept of a virtual high school was new, and he was looking for a social studies teacher that would work with a handful of students in person, but most of the work would be done virtually. I was certainly interested; it was potentially my first teaching job! After speaking to him for a few minutes, he told me that he would be in touch. However, I never heard from him again. Disappointed, I waited for more phone calls, but the calls were not coming in. My excitement for my first teaching job began to shift to discouragement. The thought that I would be subbing as much as I could while working at Applebee's was becoming more realistic.

Late July rolled around. I was working full-time with Applebee's, packing my things slowly, and still not sure what I would be doing. I was only a couple of weeks out from leaving, and neither Mary nor myself had any prospects on a job. We were frustrated, but not enough to the point that we had decided to postpone a move. Sunday, July 31 would change all of that.

I went into work for my usual 12:00 PM shift. The midday shift was one that was dictated on how busy it was. I could be there until 6:00, I could be there until 10:00, I wasn't sure. The shift started out as a typical weekend day, a lunch rush that lasted until about 2:00, a lull until about 4:30, then the dinner rush starting to pick up. During the lull, my partner on the fryer side of the kitchen and I were cleaning up from the lunch rush, restocking the fridge and freezer, and prepping for the dinner rush. My pocket began to buzz with a phone call, so I pulled it out of my pocket to see who it was. I didn't recognize the number, but I did recognize the 702 area code: this was somebody from Las Vegas calling! I got my boss' attention a few feet away and told him that I needed to take the call, to which he told me it was fine. I ducked into the walk-in cooler and answered. The voice on the other end of the phone identified himself as the principal of Desert Pines High School in Las Vegas and that he had an opening for a US History and US Government teacher, as well as a position coaching junior varsity football and asked if I was available and interested. This wasn't a call for an interview, this principal was offering me a job! For the next ten minutes, he filled me on the next steps and told me that he looked forward to meeting me in the next couple of weeks! I couldn't believe it, I had a job! I immediately called Mary, my parents, and Brandon to tell them the good news. Now the packing and preparing for the move had a purpose; I was going to be teaching in Las Vegas, not just subbing and working at Applebee's!

ON AUGUST 8, 2005, almost a year to the day when Mary and I met, we said goodbye to our friends and roommates in Marquette. With Mary driving my car, my mother sitting alongside her in the passenger seat, and me behind the wheel of a Penske moving truck with all of our possessions stuffed to the gills in the back, we left Marquette. Our destination: Iron Mountain, Michigan, a little over an hour away, where we would stay one night with Mary's family before hitting the road the next morning. As the sun was creeping over the horizon the next morning, we rolled out of Iron Mountain, crossed the Michigan border into Wisconsin, and rumbled across Wisconsin, Minnesota, Iowa, and into Lincoln, Nebraska by the end of the first day.

After a few hours of sleep, we continued our trek across Nebraska, then turned off I-80 onto I-76 into Colorado, making it to Denver in the late afternoon. While I had never seen Iowa, Nebraska, and Colorado, I was in complete awe as we started out of Denver and up into the Rocky Mountains. However, I couldn't enjoy the drive as much as I would have liked to, as driving a moving truck up those steep mountain grades was a bit nerve-wracking. Eventually, we made it to Grand Junction, Colorado after sundown, where Mary had several aunts, uncles, and cousins waiting for us. Another short night of sleep and about 500 miles of road ahead, we left early from Grand Junction to get to Las Vegas, get the keys to our apartment we had found, and move into our new home. But while the trip had been relatively smooth, the final miles would add a bit of adversity that had me questioning our decision.

As we crossed into Nevada at Mesquite, about 80 miles from Las Vegas, we topped off the gas tanks and got a snack, expecting to get to Las Vegas by early afternoon. A thunderstorm had blown through the desert a few hours earlier, making the already 110-degree heat even worse with the elevated humidity. My first thought was, "Is it going to be like this all of the time?" Not a big deal, I turned on the A/C, got onto I-15, and looked forward to the final hour or so of driving to Las Vegas. But the moving truck had other plans.

As we drove past signs that stated "NO SERVICES" off of each exit, I noticed that the temperature gauge of the truck was creeping up. I rolled down the windows and turned off the A/C, but to no avail; the truck was starting to overheat. I called Mary and my mother, driving in my car behind me, to let them know what was going on. A couple of more miles and the truck couldn't take it anymore. I pulled over on the side of the highway, popped open the hood, and realized the culprit: the radiator was BONE DRY! And again, there were no services for the next 30 miles or so. Mary and my mother drove up to the next exit, turned back toward Mesquite, and went to find coolant for the truck while I stood in the shade of the truck to avoid the heat of the Mojave Desert and asked myself if we had made a mistake in making this move. However, an hour or so later, the truck filled up with coolant and the engine's temperature back to normal, we got back on the road and into Las Vegas just before the apartment complex's office closed for the day.

This experience of adversity, in hindsight, has helped me tremendously as an educator. There is going to be adversity on a near-daily basis when working in education. It may be the unplanned fire drill that destroys your plans for a class period. It may be the Wi-Fi going down on presentation day when students are showcasing videos that they have made and posted to YouTube. It may be the tragedy of the unexpected death of a student that sends the entire school into grief mode for several days. Whatever it may be, one must

> We don't have the luxury of giving up. We need to face adversity to continue to provide our students with the best education that they deserve.

be able to adjust to adversity and not simply throw in the towel. I easily could have looked at the situation of the broken down truck, the excruciating heat, and the thought of being so far from everything I knew and simply turned back. But as educators, we don't have the luxury of giving up. We need to face adversity to continue to provide our students with the best education that they deserve, a safe place for students to learn and thrive mentally and emotionally, and use those times of adversity and turn them into those unexpected teachable moments. The teachable moment of this situation? Don't give up until you have given something a chance and make sure to double-check all of the vehicle's fluid when traveling through the desert and/or long stretches without gas stations!

FAST FORWARD 14 YEARS. Nevada is our home. Mary and I have fallen in love with the West and our Battle Born state. The beauty of the mountains and the desert, the (mostly) dry heat, the history that helped shape our country, the glitz and glamour of Las Vegas, and the friends we have made here helped our transition from everything we had known in Michigan to Nevada an easy one. I can't imagine myself anywhere else at this point in my life. And while many of the people that we had known in college were hesitant to leave, the risk that Mary and I took to try something new and make a go of it is something that I will never regret. I miss Michigan dearly at times, but it is a quick four-hour flight or three-day drive back whenever I start missing my first home.

In *Tough Truths*, Deidre Maloney highlights that every single person is afraid, even the greatest leaders, teachers, and celebrities. Everyone is afraid of something. The difference between those that are successful and those that are not is the willingness to take a risk even when they are afraid. Was I afraid after finishing up school, packing up my belongings, moving across the country to a new city with a girl that I had known for less than a year? Absolutely I was afraid! But I knew that without taking the risk and doing it, I would be running the risk of putting my life on hold for an unspecified amount of time while I waited for the perfect job to open up in my home state. To me, the potential benefits of that move far outweighed those of staying put.

Until relatively recently in the history of the world, most people never ventured much further than 50 miles from the place in which they were born, let alone moved across a state, a country, or the world. Developments in transportation and technology have changed that, where one can be in a different state or country in a matter of a few hours, rather than days, weeks, or months. Consider the following questions:

- Have you ever moved far, far away from everything you knew and considered your home? Where did you go?
- Why did you leave home? What risks were involved in your decision to leave?
- Do you have any regrets about your decision? What would you have changed if you had to make the decision to move again?
- What impact has your risk to move had on your career as an educator? If you haven't made a major move, have you ever considered one? What impact do you think that would have on your career as an educator?

Share your story and your thoughts on Twitter using #ToTheEdgeEDU!

3. IS THIS REALLY WHAT I WANT IN MY LIFE?

But now it seems, I'm just a stranger to myself
And all the things I sometimes do, it isn't me but
someone else

— *WASTED YEARS BY IRON MAIDEN*

My buddy, Mike, and I got on the escalator. We weren't in a hurry, so we rode rather than walked up. I asked him if the bar was going to be open when we got to the top. He replied that he figured if it wasn't, we could pull up a chair at the bar until the bartender showed up. After all, it was the bowling alley bar at a Las Vegas casino—the bowling alley was open 24 hours a day, and the bar connected to the bowling alley didn't have doors. It was just an open area slightly walled off from the bowling area so that you could hear the sports on the TV, instead of the sound of the ball striking pins.

As I expected, no one was there. It was only a little after 8:30 AM on a weekday, even if it was a Friday. But this wasn't just any Friday. Mike and I had called in sick to work so we could watch the United States take on Finland in the medal round of the Olympics. Shortly after we sat down, the bartender showed up, a tall guy with a Swedish accent that we knew relatively well, as we came to this bar to watch sports, bet some games, and play some darts and shuffleboard regularly. He was surprised to see us that early on a day when we were usually working, but when he realized we were there to watch hockey, and watch the US take on his country's rival, Finland, he promptly poured us each a beer and began to set up for his day.

A few hours and a 6-1 American victory later, we had had a few beers and decided to see if any of our friends would like to join us for happy hour, as work was starting to let out. They were surprised to hear from us, as they hadn't seen us at work that day, but a few joined us nonetheless to celebrate the end of the week and an American win, especially because it was sending the United States to the gold medal game a couple of days later.

And while hockey was the main reason we had called out from work, we didn't want to miss the game, there was another darker reason. I was miserable. I dreaded going to work every day. In my personal life, I was suffering from a great loss and was struggling to cope. Calling in sick to work to have beers with one of my best friends and watch Olympic hockey was a reprieve from the stress of the daily grind that I was experiencing at the time. But what really brought me to this place? Let me explain...

———

THE FIRST DAY OF SCHOOL—A day of excitement for most, but strikes fear in others (student, teacher, and parent alike). I honestly don't remember my first day of school as a teacher very well. I remember a lot of what led to the first day, but strangely, the day itself is a blur. Perhaps it was the stress of the move from Michigan to Nevada two weeks prior. Perhaps it was the work of getting the junior varsity football team ready for their first game, and the two weeks of two-a-day practices and scrimmages. Perhaps it was the stress of realizing that I was now a full-fledged adult and that it would be my first time with my own classes, not simply substituting for a teacher out on a sick day or working with a mentor teacher's classes during my student teaching. Either way, while I can remember a lot from my early career, sadly, my first day as a teacher is not one I remember well.

Before leaving Michigan, I was given a copy of *The First Days of School* by Harry & Rosemary Wong. This book is a "how-to" guide of sorts on becoming a teacher, highlighting some of the intricacies of the profession like classroom management, lesson planning, professionalism, and much more. I read it in the weeks leading up to that first day of school, with my biggest takeaway being that "the first days of school can make or break you" and that what one does or does not do will determine whether it will be an effective classroom or not. The Wongs also go on to say that teachers are rarely given any instruction on what to do during those first days of school.

It just so happened that Harry Wong was the keynote speaker for the new teacher kickoff event hosted by the school district a few days before the first day of school. In his keynote, he highlighted many points from the book, including what one does or does not do during those first few days. I listened intently, hoping to gain as much inspiration as I could so that my first days would set the stage for the year. I even got to speak with him for a few moments during a break in the festivities, having him sign my book and receiving well wishes from him.

While I don't remember much about the first day or the first few days of my teaching career, one thing I remember well: the great people who assisted me in the first few months. If you ask any teacher, most will tell you about the nightmare the first year, of the lack of sleep, the overwhelming number of meetings, phone calls to parents, lesson planning, grading, and everything else that comes with being a teacher. I can confidently state that my stress level during that first year was lower than it is for the average first-year teacher because of the people whom I had the honor of working with.

In the days leading up to that first day of school in the fall of 2005, I was in my classroom setting up the room, hanging some posters, and reading through first day and week procedures. A woman walked through the door and asked, "Are you Kyle?" I replied that I was, and she introduced herself as Alison Levy, who taught in the classroom next door and my mentor for the year. She explained to me that she would be checking in with me periodically to see how I was doing, help with any problems I was having, and to be a friendly face and ear anytime that I needed to talk. I was not aware at that point that I would be getting a mentor, but I was certainly thankful, as I was a bundle of nerves in anticipation of the first day of school. She introduced me to others in the social studies department, and many were gracious enough to offer advice, share some posters and other items for my classroom, and make me feel as welcome as possible. This was completely contrary to the words of Harry Wong; I was one of the few that were given instruction on what to do during the first days of school.

After the end of that whirlwind first week, I was invited to a happy hour by a colleague. We had met during the new teacher orientation in the weeks leading up to the start of school. I was told where to meet and that a handful of people would be there to celebrate the first week. Upon arriving, I met another person who ended up being very instrumental in my early career, Rickee Moss. Rickee was an English teacher with nearly 20 years of experience, but instead of treating me and others like just another newbie, she was someone who genuinely cared about how I was settling in, gave me some great advice on the ins and outs of the school and the profession in general, and became a great friend and karaoke partner (our go-to song almost every Friday for years was "Love Shack" by The B-52s).

I would say that my first year of teaching was very typical. I taught United States History and American Government and had to learn how to create unique lessons for both classes, although I will say that looking back on that first year, I'm not sure how unique, engaging, or innovative those lessons were and I should probably apologize to the students whom I had that first year and even into the next few; I have learned a lot since then. I coached junior varsity football and junior varsity baseball, so I had to learn the balance of lesson planning, teaching, grading, and coaching. I was the advisor for a student group called Sun Youth Forum, which was an event put on by the Las Vegas Sun newspaper that brought students from all over the Las Vegas Valley together to discuss and debate current events and their impact on students' lives. Overall, I look back and don't remember being overly stressed or questioning whether I had made the right choice of career during that first year.

My second year was even better. I had that year of experience under my belt, so a lot of the anxiety that one experiences during their first year was greatly reduced. I continued to coach football and baseball. I did not do Sun Youth Forum in that second year, choosing instead to let someone who could devote more time to it take the reins. In addition to teaching United States History and American Government, I agreed to work with a special education co-teacher in some of the classes. My co-teacher was hired through Teach for America. According to their website, Teach for America is an organization that works with school districts to bring teachers to underserved neighborhoods and provides teacher training for those individuals because most of the time, they are not teachers by trade. I remember truly enjoying the co-teaching model, and my co-teacher and I worked very well together. Unfortunately, this would only last a year because going into my third year, I was asked to teach Advanced Placement (AP) Government and Politics, along with a couple of sections of United States History.

It was during this third year that I began to question my decision to become a teacher, the impact I was making on students, and if it was something that I could continue to do for another thirty years. I cannot pinpoint any particular incident or something that stressed me to shift my thinking, although I can think of a few things that may have contributed to it.

Before I go any further, I must make a disclaimer. In no way are my words from this point further an attempt to call anybody out, judge anybody, settle some score, etc. These words are purely a hypothesis on why I began to question whether I should continue my career as an educator.

First of all, the school in which I was working served a lower-income working-class population. Because families often struggled to make ends meet, many students were working to support their families and would miss school or did not have the energy to be fully engaged in school. Many of the families living in the neighborhood did not speak English as their first language, if at all. Gang activity was prevalent in the neighborhood, which also had an impact on student attendance, engagement, and achievement.

About halfway through my first year, the principal who had hired me announced that he had accepted a position as the superintendent in another school district. My school would be run by one of our assistant principals on an interim basis until a new principal would be hired, with the possibility that the assistant principal serving in the meantime could be chosen. As a whole, our school had a great deal of respect for this individual and hoped that, in the end, he would be named principal. However, after several months, it was announced that the district would be naming another individual as the new principal. We were disappointed, but for the most part, we were open-minded to the new principal and would "give them a chance."

THE CULTURE of the school changed drastically under the new leadership. Policies on lesson planning, communication, and even dress code were radically different from before, which is to be expected when new leadership takes over. Many people did not like a lot of the new changes. The school already had a high yearly turnover rate, but after that first year under the new principal, I feel like even more teachers than usual sought positions in other schools. I even entertained the notion of going somewhere else, but not so much because of the changes in policy and culture—it was more because of the rumblings that budget cuts could potentially eliminate many positions at the school, and we would have to leave anyway. I felt that if there was a possibility that I was going to leave, I would want to have a choice in the matter, much like the young men who enlisted in the Army or Marine Corps during World War II rather than waiting for their draft notice. Ultimately, I ended up staying after reassurance that my position would be safe for the following year.

One of the changes in policy that caused me great frustration was a new grading policy, the minimum F policy. At the beginning of my third year, this policy was introduced as a way to motivate students to do better, knowing that they would always have a chance to pass classes. The idea was that if a student had 30% during the first quarter, the chances of that student passing the semester were very slim. If the score was rounded to 50%, that gave the student a better chance of passing. It also gave students that had an extenuating circumstance the chance to pass, such as a student who missed a great deal of school after a prolonged illness, a death in the family, or something similar. As it was explained, the policy made sense, but in action, flaws quickly were realized, in my opinion.

The way that the policy was implemented was that the student had the minimum F policy applied to all assignments, activities, and assessments, regardless if they had been attempted, completed, turned in, etc. rather than applied at the end of a quarter. What students quickly realized was that they did not have to put forth much of an effort at all and could still receive a D for the quarter and/or semester. On test days, many students would write their names on the test and turn it in a few seconds after receiving, telling teachers, "I'm going to take my minimum F," rather than attempting the assessment. Students did it on assignments, on projects, on anything that would be entered into the gradebook. Even students who were typically high-achieving seemed to embrace the policy and refused to complete work. They quickly realized that they could put forth a minimum effort and still pass, which is why many teachers began to call the policy the Minimum Effort Policy. When entering a minimum F score into the online gradebook, the coding would default to "MF" to indicate that the student received the minimum score of 50% for the entry, so you can probably guess how some teachers referred to it.

A lively debate could ensue regarding grading policies and how schools assess student learning, whether grades are an outdated concept, the effect of grades on students' emotional well-being, and so on. But for the sake of time, I'll just address my opinions of the minimum F policy. I am a strong believer that high expectations yield higher achievement and results. Even if one does not fully meet the expectations, results of high quality will occur by default in most cases. I firmly believe that the way that the minimum F policy, as it was implemented, resulted in sending a message to the students of my school: the school did not believe that they were capable of higher achievement, and the policy was the method of lowering the expectations. In turn, it made frustrated teachers (like myself) not put forth as much effort into planning engaging lessons, as the expectation became that regardless of what we did as teachers, students were most likely not going to engage. Staff and student morale suffered greatly during this time—whether or not the minimum F policy was a direct cause of the drop is something that I will never know. The principal voiced on several occasions that the policy would not be going away.

Another reason that I began to question whether I should continue in education was the constant micromanaging of most aspects of my role as a teacher, whether it was perceived or real. I began to feel like my freedom to present material and teach my classes was dictated by my supervisor. My required lesson plan

> I am a strong believer that high expectations yield higher achievement and results. Even if one does not fully meet the expectations, results of high quality will occur by default in most cases.

format was a tedious three-page document that, even after I got used to it, still took me nearly an hour to write for a one week lesson, and that was per subject. I felt like I was constantly being watched, and the slightest mistake would be a "Gotcha!" moment that would lead to a write-up. I began to dread going into school each day and would count-down the days to breaks, especially summer break. This made for my remaining time at this school very long, and when looking back at it now, I don't look back at much of it very fondly.

GOING INTO MY FOURTH YEAR, I decided I needed to do something that would respark my love of education. My friend Alison, my mentor from year one, and I decided to enroll in an online Master of Education (M.Ed.) program through Southern Utah University. While a pay raise was certainly a perk of completing the program (and at the time, prob-ably the main reason why we both enrolled), I also looked at it as a way to improve my practice, engage my students more, and rekindle that fire that I had once had for education. For about a year and a half between year four and year five, we completed the requirements of the program, earned our degrees, and in the process, I was able to realize that education was the right place for me and that a change of scenery may be all that I needed to really feel better about myself as an educator.

Just before finishing my degree, I applied for a social studies position at a fairly new school, East Career & Technical Academy, where some of my former colleagues from Desert Pines had transferred when it opened for the 2008-2009 school year. I interviewed with the principal and social studies department head and discussed my strengths, what I could bring to East Tech, and how I would be finishing up my degree in a few months. A week later, I was offered a position at East Tech, which I gladly accepted. The remainder of that school year was tough for many reasons, but I got through it and changed my career trajec-tory. I am where I am today as a result of that change.

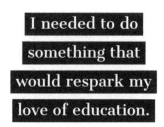

When I look back at these years of my life and my career, there is so much to unpack. I easily could have walked away. The plan that I had was to leave education and go to the police academy in Las Vegas to become a police officer in the Las Vegas Metropolitan Police Department. I don't really remember any other plans from that time because frankly, I wasn't sure what skill set I could bring anywhere else. Going all the way back to my days as a young kid, I can remember wanting to be a police officer, so it made sense to me at the time. It also crossed my mind to go to the military, but I wasn't sure how that would work. At this point, I was married, owned a home in Las Vegas, was in my late 20s, and as a result of not working out as I had for so long through all of my years of playing football, I had gained weight and was out of shape. Instead, I chose to take the risk of sticking things out and banking on trying a new school as a way to save my career.

Could this have backfired? Absolutely! I could have easily moved on to another school and realized that education was just not for me. I could have been just as miserable as I had been for years and continued on, letting my physical, mental, and emotional well-being suffer, as well as put my relationships with my wife, family, and friends at risk. Ultimately, I made the right decision; I am in a great place today because of the adversity that I went through during these years, the risk of spending thousands of dollars to further my education in hopes of jumpstarting my career and moving on to another school.

There are always going to be times in one's life where adversity in relationships, a job, or home life can become overwhelming. While it can be very hard to do, one needs to seek help for those situations. Had I sought out help, my experience in those years may have been much different. If you are faced with a similar situation, find somebody to confide in, a colleague, a department or grade level leader, an administrator, or a therapist. Sometimes, simply talking about frustrations can be helpful. It may not solve the problems, but by expressing yourself, it may relieve some of the tension and stress. And if that doesn't alleviate anything, there is no shame in looking elsewhere. You, as an educator, are at your best when you are happy in your career, and you have so much to offer students, it would be a shame if an unfavorable situation drove you from the profession like it nearly did to me.

Consider the following questions in regards to your professional and personal experiences:

- Have you ever stuck something out in hopes that it would get better, risking your mental, physical, or emotional well-being?
- What were the results of that risk? Do you have any regrets about that risk?
- If faced with a similar situation today, how would you approach it differently, knowing what you know now?
- Have you ever experienced a situation in your career as an educator that went against your principles and had a negative impact on your work? What did you do, or what could you do now to improve your situation?

Share your story and your thoughts on Twitter using #ToTheEdgeEDU!

4. RENEWED & FLOURISHING

Born to bleed fighting to succeed
Built to endure what this world throws at me

— *In Ashes They Shall Reap by Hatebreed*

For an afternoon in mid-October, it was warm, especially for the Napa Valley. The door to the classroom was wide open, as I was hoping to get some air to circulate through the room and cool it off some, especially because as more people filed in, the warmer it started to get. The notes of Canadian rock legends Rush were pumping as best as they could out of the speakers of my iPad Mini as I mingled throughout the room, introducing myself, handing out some stickers, and making small talk. It was the final session of a long two days of the Fall CUE conference, and I was about to give a presentation on the basics of Pear Deck.

I figured that as it was the last session, the number of attendees would be minuscule. After all, people had flights to catch, and the nearest airports were nearly an hour away in Oakland, San Francisco, or Sacramento. Or, like me, people had to drive home, and the majority of us, whether we were flying or driving, had to go to school the next day.

And if you have ever been to a really great conference, while you are excited to get back and implement the awesome things that you learned, they can also be exhausting. But when it was all said and done, over 50 people had popped into the room to get a few more things for the proverbial tool chest before heading home. An hour later and happy with my session and the connections that I made, I packed up my stuff, said a few goodbyes to friends old and new, and got in my car for the three-hour drive home where I would have the opportunity to reflect and decide what I should try first with my students the next day.

Now, this is a far cry from where I was when I was contemplating the police academy. How could I go from wanting to leave education altogether to connecting with educators from around the world to better my craft and to share my expertise and passion for teaching? Let's find out...

New surroundings, new colleagues, new procedures, new everything. My first day at East Career & Technical Academy was essentially like my first day at Desert Pines all over again. The only thing missing was the nervousness of meeting students for the first time. This was the start of year six, I had done this before, meeting students would be the easy part. Some of my previous colleagues were at East Tech, so getting to know people became a little bit easier. But my biggest fear? Not knowing how this would work out. I was a bit reserved considering my experiences of the previous few years. Was life at a new school going to be that much better?

My questions were answered almost immediately. East Tech was not like my previous school. The only similarity was that each school had very similar demographics: students came from unstable families, families worked multiple jobs to make ends meet, crime and gang activity were present in neighborhoods, and some students struggled with attendance for various reasons. The main difference was that East Tech was a school in which one had to apply to attend and was selected through a blind process that did not take into consideration any academic, social, and/or demographic factors. The school served the same or similar neighborhoods as my previous school, but the way students' education was delivered, and the expectations were different.

Student schedules were built based on the program area students selected. Students could select from a multitude of programs like auto mechanics, construction, medical, education, culinary arts, and marketing, just to name a few. Over the course of their four years at East Tech, students would complete core requirements in math, science, English, and social studies, electives, and courses tailored for their program to graduate with not only a high school diploma but also a skill in which they could pursue further in college, trade school, the military, or a career. Students were expected to complete many of their requirements through project-based learning and building skills in content knowledge, written communication, technology, collaboration, presentation, and problem-solving skills.

What also made East Tech different was how students were assigned to classes. All students were assigned to teachers based on their program area. Basically, a culinary arts students would have the same teachers and classmates for all subjects to promote community among students and to encourage collaboration among teachers in planning. As a result, I got to work very closely with my neighbor in the classroom next door, Jayme Rawson, who taught English. She and I were able to plan projects in a cross-curricular fashion, incorporating her English standards into my United States History standards. And I had worked with Jayme at the previous school for three years and had kept in contact; in fact, Jayme was the one who had encouraged me to apply for the position at East Tech, so I owe a lot to her, and she was an integral influence in resurrecting my teaching career.

In previous years, any new policies that were implemented were directives from above with very little to no input from the rest of the staff. At East Tech, our principal and leadership team valued our opinions and asked for feedback on any potential changes in policy. Doors were always open to voice concerns. And perhaps most important in comparison to my previous school, I felt that I had the freedom to teach and plan again, and we were expected to hold students to high expectations, expectations that most students embraced and rose to the challenge. Within months, I felt much better about my role as an educator and began to feel like I was making an impact on students once again.

After my shift to East Tech, I continued to coach football. With a year left at Desert Pines, after coaching there for four years, I accepted a coaching position at a small school nearby called Mountain View Christian School. East Tech did not have sports, so I stayed on at MVCS, working with a great group of passionate coaches and student-athletes and was fortunate enough to be a part of teams that went to the state championship game three times in four years. I also helped create the East Tech Ski & Snowboard Club after a student approached me about creating the club. For four years, my club members would fundraise and plan trips to places like Brianhead, UT, and various resorts around Lake Tahoe, participating in a sport that was not widely accessible in Southern Nevada and for many students, something that they may have never done living in the desert. I look back fondly on my times as a coach and a ski club advisor and reminisce about each frequently.

ABOUT A YEAR into my time at East Tech, I became a father for the first time. Elsa Cody Anderson was born on November 18, 2011, at 9:53 PM after my wife, Mary, was induced a day and a half earlier. Labor was slow, but the epidural did its job, as Mary, my mother, and I were playing a game of Uno about an hour before Elsa arrived. An elevated temperature caused the doctors concern, so Elsa spent a week in the neonatal intensive care unit (NICU), but between the Thanksgiving holiday and a very helpful and understanding administrative staff at my school, I was able to spend much of that time at the hospital with my Little Ladybug and Mary, then bringing her home and getting acclimated to life as a new parent.

What my time at East Tech really did for me while revitalizing my career was to help me realize that I had a lot to offer in the way of creativity and skills that I should share with my colleagues and beyond. In the past, because I did not feel that my thoughts were valued, I often kept to myself. The culture of openness at East Tech shifted my view that my knowledge, skills, and opinions were valued and worth considering. When staff development days came around, I was asked on several occasions to participate in the training, something that I had never been asked to do in previous years. Between lesson ideas, technology skills, and more, I began to open up more and share with my colleagues. I even served on the school improvement team and contributed to the team that built our accreditation application when that came due.

I began to take more risks in lessons and projects after making the move to East Tech. While the book hadn't been written yet at this point in my career, Dave Burgess' *Teach Like a Pirate* is a book that I can certainly relate to when thinking about the

> The culture of openness at East Tech shifted my view that my knowledge, skills, and opinions were valued and worth considering.

resurrection of my teaching career. The premise of this book is to engage students by infusing the PIRATE ethos: passion, immersion, rapport, ask and analyze, transformation, and enthusiasm. By incorporating these concepts into teaching, one creates a culture of learning, community, and creativity that will make students want to be in class.

Again, because *Teach Like a Pirate* did not exist yet and because I did not have the opportunity to read it until a few years later, I did not know that what I was doing was similar. Even today, while I have tried to incorporate the PIRATE ethos into my teaching, I am nowhere near the teacher that Mr. Burgess is; he is a one of a kind specimen that I can only dream to be half of in my lifetime. But his style of teaching and his book are proof that one should take risks in teaching, much like I felt safe to do upon arriving at East Tech.

Perhaps my favorite activity that I created during this time was an end of the year culminating project that I called "Dinner for the Ages," the project that I referred to at the beginning of the book. I got the basic idea for this project after attending an AP US History training one summer. (Unfortunately, I cannot recall the name of the person who planted this seed, and if you are that person and are reading this, my sincerest of thanks for helping to spur this idea!) The premise of the project is for a group of students to create a guest list of influential figures from throughout American history, invite them to a dinner party, present them with a modern-day issue (e.g., corporate profits vs. workers' compensation), write a script of a conversation of those at the table, and incorporate the views and customs of each dinner guest into the conversation to help shape how they would approach the problem.

Dinner guests ranged from presidents, military leaders, scientists, professional athletes, artists, and much more. While many of these figures were covered throughout the school year, many more were not. Either way, students had to meticulously research each historical figure and work together with their groups to create a relevant conversation that they would eventually present to their peers at a formal dinner table on the stage of our school's theater.

The purpose of this project was multifaceted. One, it was a way for students to really think outside of the box about their learning about American history from the year. History is an important subject, but what is more important is for students to think about how and why history matters. By thinking about how others would have approached problems, the project gave students a chance to think about the issues that the United States faces today.

Second, it was a great way to review and wrap up the school year. I could have easily wrapped up the year with some standard review and the final exam, but why? What is the fun in that? This was a much more engaging and creative way to review some of the key people, events, historical documents, and more that were covered during the year. However, it also went beyond simply what the standards covered; students were creative and passionate about what they thought was pertinent to the conversations that they wrote and how these concepts applied to solving modern-day problems.

Lastly, this project took advantage of the time that I still had with my students. While many students and teachers tend to shut down in the last couple of weeks of the school year, I saw this as an opportunity to use every last second that I had with my students as productive learning time. Now don't get me wrong, not every project presented was a DaVinci or a Picasso. There were certainly some duds because groups had checked out for the year. However, even the lower quality projects that were presented were much better than if I had given students a packet of review activities and turned on a few movies in the last couple of weeks of the year.

The catalyst for this shift in my mindset came from more than the welcoming environment of the school that allowed me to feel safe in taking risks in creative lessons and projects. At the beginning of the 2013-2014 school year, our school was selected by the district to pilot Google Apps for Education. Each staff member would receive a Google account that included access to Gmail, Google Drive, and a host of other Google tools. As somebody that had been toying around for several years with innovative ways to use digital tools in my lessons, I was extremely excited for this pilot program and hit the ground running, learning as much as I could about the GAFE tools and trying new things in my classroom, some very successfully, some completely falling on its face.

Word began to get out that I was becoming quite savvy with these Google tools. My colleagues would come to me with questions about how to use tools and how I implemented them in my classroom, which

I was glad to share. But it was just limited to colleagues in my school: word began to get out to people throughout the district that I was knowledgeable about the tools, so I began to get emails about various Google tools. However, even at this juncture, it still hadn't crossed my mind that I could provide professional development to large groups of people; I was just learning what I could to improve my practice, and if people asked for help, I was happy to oblige.

THE TURNING POINT came in January 2015. The school district had decided to roll out Google for the entire district, not just the pilot schools like mine. My supervisor, Tina Statucki, sent me an email from her husband, Craig, who was organizing a Google Apps for Education Summit at his school across town. He had a few free entries to the event, and Tina wanted to know if I wanted to go to the two-day event. I was certainly intrigued, as I had never heard of EdTechTeam, the organization that hosts the summits, and the fact that I had been given a voucher for a free entry to an event that cost several hundred dollars to attend. I graciously accepted the invitation to attend and can confidently say that attending this summit changed my life.

Walking into that summit, I was completely overwhelmed, but in a good way. I was surrounded by nearly 300 people that were seeking to improve their technology skills, most of whom I had never met, but could easily connect with because of our mutual love of technology. I learned right away that I was one of the few in the room that was not engaged on Twitter for professional purposes; my attitude toward Twitter was that it was a platform used for cyberbullying and celebrity gossip, not as a tool for professional development. Then there was the selection of sessions in which to choose from! Where do I go? What did I want to learn more about? The possibilities were endless.

After that weekend and a conversation with Craig Statucki, the organizer of the event, after swearing I would never do it, I created a Twitter account. I even let my students have a say in what my handle would be. A lot of them said that I knew a lot of random things about history (I do) and could tell a lot of long-winded stories surrounding the random things that I knew (I can). After creating a short list of Twitter handles, my students and I settled on @AndersonKnowsIt.

I hadn't been on Twitter for very long when I had the first incident involving the platform with one of my students. I had a strict personal policy that I would not follow students back on Twitter, even if they followed me. I wanted to keep the account as professional as possible, and let's face it: teenagers will state things verbally and through social media that does not fit the description of professional. One day early in the school year, I posted a question on Twitter for my students to discuss if they chose to do so. One of my students posted her response and had a few others respond back to her. I clicked on the tweet to read the rest of the thread and noticed her profile picture was, to put it delicately, not very school appropriate. This young lady had chosen to post a photo of herself with several cigars in her mouth while holding two large bottles of beer and have even posted a caption that described that she was using illegal substances, even for adults (this was before Nevada's passage of a law that allows for adults over the age of 21 to use cannabis). I had to report it to the school administration, to which they dealt with it accordingly. However, this opened up a lesson for me in regards to my risk of using social media with students.

This was a clear cut example of a student who would have benefited from a series of lessons in digital citizenship. Jennifer Casa-Todd, in her book, *Social LEADia*, highlights a plethora of reasons why students and teachers should be engaged in social media in the classroom, the importance of digital citizenship and the digital footprint that every person possesses, how the positives in our lives can drown out the negativity posted on social media, and the impact that social media will continue to have on education in the future. I wish I would have had access to this book, or something similar, before engaging my students in social media in the classroom. Perhaps I would have been prepared to take the risk of using social media in my classroom. Perhaps this young lady would not have to learn this lesson in digital citizenship in the manner in which she did; perhaps she would have made a better decision in her choice of what she posted on social media. However, since reading *Social LEADia*, I am much better prepared to engage my students using social media and understanding how students use social media in their daily lives; the risk isn't as crazy as a result!

In the beginning, my Twitter account was focused mainly on communicating with my students, following other educators, participating in a few Twitter chats, and tweeting out "this day in history" kind of things. I quickly began to realize that Twitter was going to be much more than that for me. Today, I don't use Twitter much for interacting with current students. (Some of my students from a few years ago who followed me in the days, weeks, and months after I created the account still communicate with me on Twitter; it's really nice to hear and see what they are doing with their lives in the years since I have had them as students.) My focus now is to connect with other educators, learn from them, and share my expertise on various subjects as a way to develop my professional skills. Since the focus of my account has shifted, my handle's name has shifted too, from @AndersonKnowsIt to @AndersonEdTech (and a whole brand has emerged from that as well, more on this later).

Perhaps the best thing to happen the weekend of that Google Summit though was the people that I met, in particular, a man named Lucas Leavitt. At lunch on the first day, I sat with Tina, and she introduced me to Lucas. He was the Google administrator for the school district, overseeing every Google account for every employee and student in the district. (This was no small feat, as there were over 300,000 students and over 20,000 employees.) He informed me that he had heard my name in various circles regarding my Google skills and asked if I would be interested in presenting at some district events in the future as more people would require training in the Google universe. Nervously, I accepted his invitation, not knowing exactly what it entailed. Lucas informed me that he and his team would be in touch shortly.

That near future came very quickly. An individual from the district who was tasked with organizing a Google "mini-conference" contacted me a few days later and asked me if I would be willing to present a couple of sessions on the basics of Google Classroom. He informed me that Google Classroom was one of the most requested topics for the event, as it had been introduced by Google a few months prior and that according to multiple sources, I was proficient in its use and understood its intricacies. This was going to be my first ever presentation to teachers in which I was the sole presenter, and I would not know most of the attendees; the nerves certainly began to kick in, and I knew that I would have to create a presentation that would really knock it out of the park.

I set out right away, putting together my presentation. Because many of the attendees were going to be brand new to Google Classroom, I knew that I was going to need to make the session as visual and hands-on as possible. TechSmith Snagit's Chrome extension was my best friend in building this session in Google Slides, as I incorporated numerous screenshots of what users would be seeing as they dived into Google Classroom (this Chrome extension is no longer available, but I highly recommend purchasing TechSmith's Snagit program or heading to the Chrome Web Store to install a similar screenshot extension like Awesome Screenshot or Nimbus). I even incorporated a few animated GIFs (with a hard G, a soft G makes it a brand of peanut butter, but I digress). After several hours of preparing the presentation, I felt like I was ready for the event.

On the day of the event, I was informed at check-in that I would be presenting the session twice: once in the morning and once in the afternoon. I ventured over to the classroom where I would be presenting and realized that I did not have the proper equipment to hook up my computer to the projector. Today, I have an entire section of my computer bag devoted to adapters, or dongles as we like to call them in the presentation circuit. But at the time, I had a standard HDMI cable, but the projector was a VGA. I asked around to see if anybody had the adapter I needed, but to no avail. My last bet was to ask the person presenting in the room before me if they had the adapter needed. It was at this moment I really began to get nervous.

When I walked into the room just before his session to ask the presenter, he was in the process of setting up his computer, a set of portable speakers, and a microphone headset that he would use during the presentation. I didn't have any of this, so now I was wondering if people were going to take me seriously. He also didn't have the dongle I needed, but he assured me that I could use his computer for my presentation. That made me feel a little better, but as the minutes disappeared before my presentation, I began to get even more nervous.

Finally, the time had come: I was about to present my first session to a group of adult learners. I had no idea how many people would be there or if they would take me seriously since I was not nearly as prepared as the previous presenter. As attendees began to trickle in, I began to freak out on the inside. First, it was about ten people, then twenty. It was like a clown car at the circus, the stream of people didn't seem to be slowing or stopping! The room was filling up to standing room only capacity! When it was all said and done, I had over FIFTY people in the room for my first ever session. But there was no turning back, it was time to make it happen. (Remember Deidre Maloney's lesson that everybody is afraid, but they do it anyway? Here was one of those moments!)

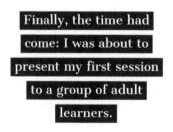

I nervously introduced myself to the attendees and the topic of the session, encouraging those in the room to stop me at any time and ask questions about the material. As I began to dive into the first few slides, my nerves slowly dissipated. My audience was engaged, they were asking great questions, and I relaxed, realizing that I had worried over nothing at all. An hour later, I had several people stick around to ask further questions and exchange contact information for future questions. After lunch, I presented the session again to a much smaller audience, but because I had gotten the proverbial monkey off of my back, the second session was much smoother, and I felt much more confident in my ability to present to adults.

When I look back on this now, it's hard to believe that I was so nervous. Shortly after that presentation in February 2015, I presented at a similar event hosted by my district. Then it was announced that my school would be hosting an EdTechTeam Google Summit and that they were looking for local presenters. My supervisor, Tina, encouraged me to apply, to which I agreed and was accepted!

Amid the excitement of discovering this new passion, Mary and I were expecting our second child. On April 23, 2015 at 9:22 AM, Reed Robert Anderson arrived. He was a lot different than his older sister. Labor for Reed was only a few hours. His vitals were solid upon birth, so a stay in the NICU was not going to be necessary. In fact, Mary and Reed were doing so well that fewer than 24 hours after his arrival, we were cleared to go home. Mary's stay at the hospital was fewer than 48 hours, including admittance, induction, birth, and recovery. Elsa was excited to be a big sister, and my parents and Mary's mother were excited that there were a granddaughter and a grandson!

Today, I live for presenting at conferences. I have now presented at dozens of school, district, regional, and even national events. I have met hundreds of amazing people and made authentic professional connections with these educators. Many of them have even become very good friends, regardless of the distance between us. I owe all of this to several risks that I took over the course of a few years: the risk of putting myself out there with my colleagues, attending that first Google Summit, creating my Twitter account, presenting at that district "mini" conference," and applying to present at the Google Summit hosted at my school. Without these risks, where would I be today? I can almost guarantee my career would look a lot differently, and I wouldn't know nearly what I know now or the people that have influenced me over the years and into the future.

Many people state that presenting to adults is a lot different than presenting to students for various reasons. At some point in an educator's career, they will have to present to a group of adults, whether it be to an interview panel after applying for a job, providing professional development to fellow educators in one's school, district, or beyond, or giving a keynote address to hundreds of people to kick off a conference. In reflecting on your experience as a presenter beyond teaching students, consider the following questions:

- What was your first experience as a presenter like? Think about what led to you that first presentation, how you prepared, your feelings leading up to it and during the presentation, etc.
- What is your experience now as a presenter? Have you modified how you prepare for a presentation in comparison to that first one? How do you debrief after presenting and learn from your experience?
- If you've never presented, is there something specific that may be holding you back? What do you think it will take to have you make the leap into the presentation universe?

Share your story and your thoughts on Twitter using #ToTheEdgeEDU!

5. LEADERSHIP?

Sometimes, I feel the fear of uncertainty stinging
    clear
And I can't help but ask myself how much I'll let
    the fear
Take the wheel and steer
It's driven me before
And it seems to have a vague, haunting mass
    appeal
But lately, I am beginning to find
That I should be the one behind the wheel

— DRIVE BY INCUBUS

The excitement was thick. After 13 grueling weeks, countless written assignments, hundreds of pages read, numerous in-class discussions, and even having to wear a suit while sitting in uncomfortable plastic chairs for hours at a time (in a room where the air conditioning may or may not be working), it was our last night. My classmates and I mingled with one another, relieved to be finished with the class, and snacking on cookies that were provided. We had a few minutes to chat amongst ourselves before some of the "higher-ups" in our district came to address us, congratulate us on completing the class, and presenting us with our certificates of completion.

But after the festivities and the kind words, we still had work to do, so the class wasn't technically over. Another couple of hours of reading, discussion of scenarios that one may encounter on a typical day in a school, and a few tips on the next steps now that we were finished with the class, and then we were finally done. I stuck around for a few minutes after class was over to chat with a couple of my colleagues in the parking lot, asking them what they thought they would do next. Would they stay in the classroom for a while longer, or were they going to dive right in and pursue their first job as an administrator? Me, I wasn't sure what I was going to do.

I've never considered myself a leader. Throughout my childhood and adolescence, I was never the team captain or usually looked to for advice on much of anything. I never really considered myself a follower either, so for most of my life, I was trapped in some sort of purgatory between a shepherd and a sheep. That continued into college and in the early years of my teaching career. It wasn't until I had been at East Tech for a few years that I began to realize that many considered me to be a leader, and my mindset began to shift, a mindset that forced me to seek out leadership opportunities rather than sit back and observe.

While so much of my previous mindset was shaped by my shy, introverted personality of my youth, even after I opened up and became the extroverted "social butterfly" that I am today, I still didn't think that what I thought mattered to those in charge. I had thoughts about things in small circles, but never had the guts to necessarily voice those thoughts to larger groups or directly to the leaders in my life. I also looked at leadership as something that was the right fit for some people, but certainly not for me. As a young educator, I can distinctly remember thinking that one could not pay me enough to be in a position of leadership, emphasizing how much one had to go through to be a leader. And many of the leaders in my life in my early days weren't what I would refer to as inspiring leaders, ones that motivated others to become leaders themselves.

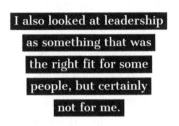

The principal and the assistant principals at East Tech were different. They sought feedback and opinions from teachers. They recognized the good things that were happening in the classroom and offered constructive criticism for things in which one could improve upon rather than a reprimand. And it was my principal, Glenda Goetting, and assistant principal, Tina Statucki, who helped to shift my thoughts on leadership, inspiring me to strive to be more of a leader.

In early 2013, the thought first crossed my mind about my future in education as an administrative leader. Not that I was bored with the classroom and teaching social studies, far from it! My career had been resurrected at this point, and I was in love with my career, but I am always looking for a challenge. I decided to begin researching some graduate programs to complete the requirements for an administrative endorsement.

My focus was mostly on programs that were completed online, as I had already completed my Master's degree online and enjoyed the flexibility of the program. After reviewing a few different programs, I ultimately settled on a program offered by Nova Southeastern University, a school based out of Florida with a solid reputation for online learning. It also didn't hurt that they offered a discount for employees of my district. The program was an educational specialist degree program, a step above a master's program but below a doctoral program. And another appealing factor to the program: the entire program would take a little less than twelve months. It would certainly be time-consuming and demanding, but I was willing to put forth the effort to get it done and have another option available for advancement in my career.

OVER THE NEXT 11 MONTHS, I plugged away at the 36-credit program. The courses were set up so that I took two classes at a time for about six weeks. Once I was done with coursework, I had an internship of 300 hours of experience in an administrative setting. During this time, I had to observe and perform a variety of school administrative functions, such as supervising students during lunch or on field trips, student discipline, teacher observation and evaluation, and budgeting and scheduling. The bulk of my hours were spent in the supervision of students and student discipline, since the first step into administration in my district was to, most likely, go the route of a secondary dean of students, a position that primarily handles discipline.

As I began to get close to finishing the program in the spring of 2014, I contemplated what I would do once I finished. Would I start applying for administrative positions and leave the classroom? Would I search for my perfect administrative position and apply only if it came along? Or would I put my degree in my pocket and hold onto it for a while and continue to serve students in the classroom? Several factors contributed to making my decision for me, the decision that I would be staying in the classroom for the foreseeable future.

First, there was a delay in conferring my degree. I finished up all of my coursework in May, anticipating that my degree would be posted by the beginning of June. For reasons that I do not recall, my degree took a little bit longer to post, which delayed my ability to submit my transcripts and application to the State of Nevada to add school administration to my teaching license. Without the endorsement on my license, I could not apply for the administration applicant pool in my district.

A few weeks later, my degree was confirmed. I received my diploma and transcripts and submitted my application for my administrative endorsement to the State of Nevada. Then I contacted the school district about how to apply for the administrative pool. The person whom I spoke to was very nice, very helpful and quickly emailed me a link to the online application, informing me to complete it, submit the necessary documentation, and to watch my email for instructions after my application was approved. I was informed that it could take several weeks, so when those several weeks turned into a couple of months, I didn't think twice about it; I was enjoying teaching, so I wasn't in any hurry to leave the classroom.

After those couple of months, my supervisor, Tina Statucki—the person who was able to help open numerous doors for me professionally—casually asked me if I had applied for the pool. Tina had also been my mentor during my administrative internship, so she had a vested interest in my success, not just as a teacher, but as a potential administrative candidate as well. When I told her that it had been several weeks and I hadn't heard anything, she advised me to contact the district again to see what was going on because, in her words, there was no way that it should have taken that long.

I contacted the district later that day to inquire about my application to the pool. As it turns out, the person who previously had helped me had given me the link to the teacher pool, not the administrative pool. Essentially, I had completed an application to enter into the teacher transfer pool, a pool that I was already a part of but now had an up-to-date profile if I was interested in transferring to another school in the district. The person who helped me this time apologized several times for the mistake. While I could have been very frustrated, again, I wasn't necessarily in a hurry to leave the classroom. I thanked her, completed the form, and within a couple of days, I received an email that I had been accepted into the pool and was now able to apply for administrative positions available in the district.

The Clark County School District was unlike most other districts around the country. Rather than filling administrative positions at the beginning of the school year, more often than not, positions started immediately. That said, a person could accept a position as a dean of students in October, nearly two months into the school year, creating an opening in their teaching position. However, teaching positions would be filled during the year as well; if a position couldn't be filled, a long-term substitute would fill the position until a full-time replacement could be hired or in the case of an opening due to a promotion, resignation, etc.

By the time I was accepted into the pool, the end of the school year was quickly approaching. The last thing that I wanted to do was to leave my students and my school with a few weeks left, so I didn't even bother to look for positions. My thought was that I would start looking to see if anything was available in the summertime or possibly at the beginning of the next school year in the fall. However, this decision would delay obtaining an administrative position even further.

Before 2015-2016, for several years, the basic requirements to apply for administrative positions in the Clark County School District were to have served as a teacher for a minimum of three years, have completed a school administration degree program through an accredited college or university, add the school administration endorsement to your teaching license, and apply for the pool. Upon acceptance, you were free to apply for administrative positions for which you were qualified and interested in obtaining. The requirements for applying for positions would be changing, starting in the fall of 2015.

Many years prior, before a teacher could enter the administrative ranks, one would also need to complete a district leadership academy. This academy would prepare a teacher for the rigors of administration through a series of classes and job shadowing, rather than throwing one into the lake and hoping that they could swim. The school district had abandoned the academy when there was a critical shortage of administrators due to the number of new schools that were opening each year. With growth slowing, it was decided by district brass that it would be best to resurrect the academy to better prepare administrative candidates.

I first learned of this change from my principal, Glenda. Even though I had already applied and been accepted to the pool, I was not going to be eligible to apply for positions because I had not completed the leadership academy. District teachers were notified that more information would be forthcoming regarding the leadership academy, the requirements to apply for the academy, etc. Glenda told me that as soon as the application window opened, I needed to submit my application, so I had a chance to be accepted.

There were several steps in the process of acceptance into the leadership academy. First, a standard application, including a cover letter, transcripts, teaching license, etc. Upon submitting the application, if you made the cut, you would be invited to conduct a timed writing task. You would only know what to write about when you arrive at the scheduled time for the writing. Then lastly, if your writing was deemed sufficient, you would be invited to a panel interview where you would be asked a series of questions similar to those asked in the interview process of an administrative position.

After submitting the application, it was a couple of weeks before I heard back. I received an email stating that my application had been accepted and that I needed to report to a middle school across town about a week later for the writing task. Since the leadership academy and the application process were new, I didn't even have someone I could ask about what to expect. A couple of administrators at my school assured me that whatever the task was that I would be fine and that I had nothing to worry about. So frankly, I didn't think about it much.

On my scheduled day and time, I reported to Johnston Middle School in North Las Vegas to complete my writing task. We were given instructions on how to complete the task by writing it in Microsoft Word, identifying our work by typing in our candidate identification number rather than our name, printing it, and submitting it to those overseeing the process. For the sake of protecting the integrity of the leadership academy's process, I won't say what I had to write about.

However, after finishing, I was confident that I had done well. Timed writing tests have never bothered me; in fact, I would rather do a timed writing test or write a research paper over a multiple-choice exam. I was informed that it would take a couple of weeks to review each candidate's writing and that we would be notified if we would be moving on to the next step of the process.

A couple of weeks later, I received another email. This email congratulated me on making it through the writing task and that I was now invited to a panel interview to determine if I would be invited to participate in the leadership academy. While the email did not say what I would be asked about in the interview, it did say that it would be a process of no more than 15 minutes. To prepare, I asked the administrators at my school if they would be willing to give me some tips on the process (in hindsight, I would have asked if they could conduct a mock interview with me), which they were glad to provide.

ON THE DAY of my interview, it was a cold and rainy day in Las Vegas. The streets were starting to flood in places, as rain in the desert doesn't have anywhere to go. Because I did not want to be late, I made sure to leave with plenty of time for the drive to the interview location. I ended up arriving about 45 minutes before my scheduled time, so I sat in the car for a few minutes and listened to the rain as it pounded on the roof of the car and the windshield for a few minutes to ease my mind and relax. About 20 minutes before my time, I sprinted across the parking lot (not an easy feat in a pair of dress shoes on wet pavement) and signed in, waiting to be called for my panel.

In the days and minutes leading up to my interview, I couldn't help but think about the words of George Couros in his book *The Innovator's Mindset* (2015). At one point, Mr. Couros speaks about strength-based leadership and how organizations have a more positive culture when leaders focus on a team's strengths rather than harping on improving weaknesses (Mr. Couros stresses that this does not mean that weaknesses are ignored; it just means that strengths are the focal point instead). When I read these words, it really resonated with me that in my experience, I felt more connected to my school when leaders took this approach. I decided that I wanted to weave this kind of a focus into my own leadership abilities, and if it came up in my interview, I wanted to stress the importance of my strengths and my belief in strength-based leadership.

When I was called into the interview room, I was surprisingly calm. I had put it into my mind that no matter what I was asked, I just had to answer to the best of my ability, not try to "fluff up" my responses, but be straight and to the point, and ulti-mately, if I wasn't selected, there would be another chance in the future. The panel, two principals from the district, instructed me that I would have 15 minutes to answer five questions, questions that were printed out and given to me to refer back to if needed. I would also be notified when I had five minutes left.

The timer started, and I was asked my first question. From this point forward, everything is a blur to me. I do not remember the questions, I do not remember what I said, I do not remember if I mentioned strength-based leadership. I do remember telling a story about a young man whom I had in my first year at East Tech that was very memorable to me and made an impact on me as a teacher and as a human.

This young man, whom we will call Robert, came to me on the first day of school and told me about how he struggled mightily with reading and writing and how he didn't think that he would be able to meet the demands and expectations of my class, but that he promised he would be one of the hardest working students that I would have that year. I told him that he didn't need to worry and that I was going to work with him to not only keep up in class, but also to improve his reading and writing so that he would become more proficient and pass his proficiency exams, which were a requirement for graduation at the time. My teaching partner, Jayme, would have him in her English class, so she and I discussed how we would help this young man to achieve his goals.

Fast forward two years later, Robert not only kept pace in our classes and passed them, but he was able to pass his proficiency exams ON THE FIRST ATTEMPT! Many students failed one or more of these exams on the first attempt, but Robert was able to pass his reading and writing exams and guarantee graduation. He had improved his skills in reading and writing by several grade levels during this time as well. I fondly remember shaking his hand at graduation and seeing the sparkle in his eyes as he thanked me for my support. The last time I saw Robert was a few years ago at one of the district's elementary schools where he had gotten a job as a custodian while he went to college part-time. I would love to know where this young man is now and the great things that he is doing in his life.

As I said, the interview was a blur. Before I knew it, I had answered each of the five questions, and the panel asked me if I had any questions for them. I thanked them for their time and exited the room, heading back to my car through the hallway of the school and out into the pouring rain. I got in the car, turned the key over, and turned on the wipers, confident that I had done well until I realized that I had never been notified of "five minutes left," meaning that I had taken less than 10 minutes to answer the questions. Now my stomach was in knots. Did I just blow my chance at the leadership academy? Were my answers good enough, even though I didn't take that much time? And now I was going to need to wait a month to find out. However, by the time I got home, I relaxed and told myself once again that if I didn't get in, there would be another opportunity.

Shortly after the interview, school went into winter break. After the grind of several months, teachers and students would have a couple of weeks off to recharge, spend time with family, and prepare for the second half of the school year. I didn't give the leadership academy much thought during the break, focusing instead on my family and watching as much football and hockey that I could. And once the break was over, I still didn't think about it much, as now the focus was finishing up the last couple of weeks of the semester before midterm exams.

One day after school, about a month after the interview, I got home and did the usual things: took my bags in the house, changed out of my work clothes, and went out to the mailbox to check the mail. In the mail was an envelope addressed to me with a return address from the school district. It wasn't the right size for it to be tax information, so I assumed immediately that it was information about the academy. Without waiting to go back into the house, I ripped open the envelope at the mailbox and frantically unfolded the letter. The very first word after "Dear Mr. Anderson," was "Congratulations!" I had been accepted to the leadership academy! The letter included instructions for the next steps and the schedule for the academy, which would meet on Thursday nights for the next few months.

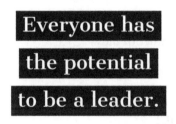

I was ecstatic! I had worked very hard for the past couple of years to get to the next step of my career, and the pieces were starting to fall into place. It also made me realize that my doubts were all for naught. In *Tough Truths* (2012), Deidre Maloney states that great leaders possess "supreme, undying confidence" in themselves and their abilities. While some may interpret this as a way of saying that great leaders are cocky or conceited, I interpret it more as a way of saying that one should be more confident and not have doubts about their ideas, abilities, or other areas.

AT THE BEGINNING of this chapter, I mentioned that I had never considered myself as a leader. If you are reading this, perhaps there is a chance that you don't consider yourself a leader either. However, everyone has the potential to be a leader. As an educator, you lead your students every day, guiding them to be amazing people. You are working with your colleagues to devise ways to better reach your students. You are a leader in your community, and while it may not seem like it at times, your community looks to you as a leader. Leadership is not simply reserved for the administrators of your school or district. And while I was inspired by some incredible leaders in my life, this does not mean that you will be inspired to pursue an administrative position. But know that you are a leader and you have amazing things to share with your colleagues and inspire people daily.

Think about your leadership skills and level of confidence while considering these questions:

- Do you consider yourself a leader? Why or why not?
- Who has been your inspiration to be more of a leader in your position? What has this person (or persons) done to inspire you?
- What draws the line between confidence and cockiness? Have leaders in your experience fallen into either of these categories?

Share your story and your thoughts on Twitter using #ToTheEdgeEDU!

6. CHANGES

Ch-ch-ch-ch-changes
Turn and face the strange
Ch-ch-changes

— *CHANGES BY DAVID BOWIE*

The phone rang, cutting into the laughter that was quite common between my office mate and I. We were always joking around, and today was no different. We had to pass the time of cleaning out our office somehow. Fifteen years of clutter had built up in the room, with items ranging to old computers, broken printers, a stack of blank video cassettes. We even found an old overhead projector, and surprisingly, it worked when we plugged it in and turned it on. It even made for a great prank that day involving our supervisor.

Earlier in the day, our supervisor had asked my colleague and me to set up a computer, projector, and speakers for a presentation that he had to give to the staff of the school on state testing that would be happening soon. It was the first time he had been in charge of testing, and he wanted to make sure that everything went smoothly for the training, so he asked that once we had it set up to let him know so he could come to check it out and make sure his presentation would work with the setup.

After setting everything up that he requested, we decided to bring in the overhead projector and set it up in the room as well. We wrote a note on the screen that the overhead was the best that we could come up with and that he was going to need to print his presentation on transparencies. Totally and completely lame, but our supervisor was about the same age as we were, so we knew he would appreciate us finding an old overhead and having a little fun. The joke got even better when we tracked him down and told him that he needed to come to check out the setup immediately, as there was a problem. I almost felt bad for a second when I saw the look of fear on his face, wondering what the issue was going to be.

My colleague and I led our supervisor to the classroom where he would be holding his presentation. We struggled to stifle our laughter as we rounded the corner and walked into the room. Within a couple of seconds, our supervisor saw the overhead and our message, turned to us and said something that I won't repeat here before the three of us burst into laughter.

But now the phone was cutting into our jokes. I figured it was either a teacher asking for some help with a program or perhaps my supervisor with some last-second requests for his training. Instead, it was my principal. He instructed me to come to his office immediately. Confused, I left my office and made my way downstairs to the office, knocked softly on the partially open door and said, "You wanted to see me?" I had no idea what was going on, whether this was good or bad.

My principal handed me his phone and said that there was somebody on the other end that needed to speak to me. Even more confused (I mean, couldn't he have transferred the call to my office?), I took the phone from him and put it to my ear and said, "Hello, this is Mr. Anderson." The voice on the other end identified herself as a principal at a middle school across town, a principal whom I had recently interviewed with for an opening at her school as the dean of students. She proceeded to inform me that after discussing with the rest of her administrative team, she wanted to offer me the position of dean of students. I was absolutely floored, but within a second or two, I collected myself and told her that I accepted. I then asked her when I would be starting, thinking that it would be a couple of weeks, at least. She asked, "Can you start on Friday?" It was Wednesday afternoon, giving me the rest of that day and Thursday to pack my belongings and prepare for a new position, one I had never done before, and in the middle of the school year to boot. Let's do a quick rewind to see what brought me to this moment.

It is year ten of my teaching career. I am at a really great place in my career, teaching United States History, advising the ski and snowboard club of my school, getting more involved in providing professional development in my district and beyond, and I have just been accepted to the leadership academy in my district as the next step in pursuing a leadership role. Things were most definitely looking up.

In her 2017 book, *Social LEADia*, Jennifer Casa-Todd talks extensively about the importance of a positive digital footprint and using social media in a positive, professional fashion. It was at about this point that I truly began to embrace social media as an agent for good. I had been on Twitter for about a year, and in the course of following other educators, I had been embracing ideas that I saw on the platform and began to implement them in my classroom, even taking the concept of Twitter chats and using them with my students, amongst tons of other great ideas.

Casa-Todd also talks about writing for an authentic audience through blogging. While she was referring more to students in the book, it was about this time that I decided to start blogging again, this time as a professional endeavor to get my thoughts out to the world and, hopefully, connect with others professionally.

Early on in my teaching career, I had a blog on Myspace. I used this blog to review and reflect on the football games that I coached on Friday nights. As a coaching staff, we would always get up early on Saturday while thoughts were still fresh in our head to go to school, watch film from the night before, and reflect on what we did well and what we needed to do to improve the next week. Later in the morning, the team would come to school to watch film, and we, the coaching staff, would share our insight into the previous night's game.

I would wake up even earlier to write my blog post. I wrote it in a first-person format, but when it was all said and done, it was essentially a newspaper story of the game. I never felt comfortable sharing it with anyone directly. I would just post it to Myspace and whomever I was connected with on the app that happened to read it, I was content with that. I wrote it every week during the football season, then occasionally throughout the school year, but I didn't take it very seriously, and eventually, I stopped writing the blog when I closed my Myspace account and created a Facebook account instead. Sadly, I do not have access to any of those old posts. I would love to go back and see what I had written all those years ago!

As I began to take more of a leadership role in my school and became involved in providing professional development, I decided that a blog would be a great way to share my expertise and thoughts. Many of the people that I was working with regularly in my district were blogging, and some of the members of the board for CUE-NV were also blogging, so I decided that if they were doing it, why shouldn't I? So in late 2015, I created a blog on Blogger and began to post periodic musings about things happening in my classroom, tools that I loved using, and much more. I eventually bought a domain, and my blog lives on today as andersonedtech.net, a blog that I still post to frequently.

CUE-NV has probably been the most important risk that I have taken in my professional career. I had heard of CUE and CUE-NV about the time that I started presenting at district functions, but I never learned much about it until the fall before I started the process for the leadership academy. Craig Statucki, the same gentleman who had given me a free entry to the Google Summit, was helping CUE to host their Rockstar event at his school and offered me a free entry to this event as well. For three days, I had the opportunity to learn from some absolute rockstars in education (hence the name, CUE Rockstar!). I also got to know Steven New, a teacher that worked at my school that I had no idea was also a "nerd like me."

After the Rockstar event, Steve informed me that he served on the board of CUE-NV, the local affiliate for CUE, Inc., an organization that seeks to connect educators and provide high-quality professional development for its members. Steve asked me if I would be interested in joining the board to help plan events for CUE-NV, since he felt that I could bring a lot of great ideas to the table. Knowing that this could expand my professional learning network further and it was something that I knew I would enjoy, I excitedly accepted his invitation and agreed to attend the next board meeting that would be held about a month later.

Since that first board meeting in the fall of 2015, I moved up from assisting the board in planning events to election as vice president of the organization, a position that I served in for about 3 and a half years until I stepped down to focus more on my family and other professional endeavors. I got to work with an amazing team of volunteers to bring high-quality professional development to educators in the State of Nevada and beyond, and I met hundreds of passionate people, many of whom have become great friends.

To say that I had found a passion for educational technology and for being a connected educator would be an understatement. That's why it seemed natural to me when I learned that there would be openings for digital learning coaches in my school district to find out more about it. A digital learning coach, a teacher on special assignment (TOSA), in many places around the country, would be assigned to a handful of schools to assist teachers in effectively implementing technology into their lessons. A DLC would visit each school at least once a week and present to teachers before or after school, set up office hours to have teachers request to meet at their convenience, and observe teachers to help provide feedback on how they can improve their practice by implementing technology.

I knew a few teachers who were serving in the digital learning coach role. I also had gotten to know the director of the department over the coaches through the district trainings that I had been presenting at. I picked their brains to see if the position was something that I would be interested in pursuing, and right away, I knew I wanted it. So as soon as the application window opened, I put in the application and waited to hear back.

Mind you, during this time, I was also going through the leadership academy in which I had been accepted a few months prior. The academy was three hours every Thursday evening. In addition to my regular day and everything that came with it, I had assignments to complete for the academy. Each week had a different theme, such as student discipline, special education law, teacher observation and evaluation, and many other topics pertinent to the role of a school administrator.

As I was completing the academy, I began to contemplate what I would do after the academy was finished. I questioned whether I was really ready to go into administration. I knew that administration was a demanding job, but the academy was really opening my eyes to what the position entailed. Part of me felt that if I wasn't 100% committed to completing the academy and pursuing an administration position, I would be letting down my instructors and would be looked upon as "that guy that wasted one of the academy's slots," but the other part of me felt that it was my life and if I didn't think I was ready for administration, then so be it.

Because of these thoughts and doubts that were creeping in, but having such a passion for technology and professional development, I decided that I would accept a digital learning

I knew that administration was a demanding job, but the academy was really opening my eyes to what the position entailed.

coach position if I was offered one or I would stay in the classroom for the time being. After all, I still loved what I was doing, but at the same time was looking for a new challenge. I even went as far as telling the instructor of the leadership academy that I had made this decision, something that was quite risky considering that the instructor could have an influence on any potential hiring in the future. However, my instructor was supportive of my decision and, while disappointed, stated that it was better for me to wait and be sure rather than dive into something that I had doubts about.

A few weeks after submitting the application for the digital learning coach position, I was contacted for an interview opportunity. I was instructed to come prepared for a standard interview panel and to present a lesson on a piece of technology, a tool, or a lesson that incorporated technology. Since I had interviewed for the leadership academy only a few months prior and technology "was my jam," I had no concerns about the interview and was very confident going into it.

The interview was quick and to the point. The panel of three asked me a handful of questions and asked me if I was prepared with a short presentation. I told them that I had a quick presentation on Remind, a communication application that allows teachers to communicate safely with students and families via phone and computer. I had been using the app to send my students reminders for quizzes and tests, due dates, etc. and I also used it with my ski and snowboard club to communicate club news and when we were at resorts. It's a much easier and safer alternative than giving out your personal phone number. I was given three minutes to make my pitch about Remind, three minutes that I used until the very last second. The panel thanked me for my time and informed me that they would be in touch.

A few days later, I received an email with an offer for a position as a digital learning coach. I replied immediately with my acceptance, and I had already decided that if offered, it was what I wanted to do. The email also notified me that more information on what schools I would be assigned to would be forthcoming, as well as when I would be able to pick up my district-issued laptop. I was also added to a Google Hangout chat of current and newly hired DLCs, where we could ask questions and exchange ideas for use in our roles as coaches.

Then it hit me. I was no longer going to be in a classroom. I had less than two months until the end of the school year before I would be a "man without a country." I realized that packing up wouldn't mean putting things in boxes to move to another room or school, but to put into my garage, in storage, or just to give away, as a lot of my stuff I would no longer need. I have never been much of a packrat, so I decided to give away as much as I could. As the weeks dwindled and the end of the school year approached, I gave away a lot of things, such as posters, art supplies, a collection of AP US History materials to the teacher that would be taking my place, and much more.

Before I knew it, the last few days of school had crept up on me. My room was virtually empty, my students knew that I would not be returning in the fall, and I had started to say my goodbyes to colleagues that I had worked with for several years. Shortly

after giving a final exam and dismissing my students on the second to last day of school for students, I received an email from the department that oversaw the digital learning coaches, stating that I needed to attend a mandatory meeting later that day at the department's office across town. At this point, I hadn't learned what schools I would be working with or received my laptop, so I assumed that this is what the meeting would be about.

My thoughts couldn't have been further from the real reason why dozens of people were called to a meeting on such short notice. As the meeting commenced, we all realized right away that something was wrong. The director of the department would barely look at us as he introduced one of the directors of the human resources department. We were then informed that due to a budget shortfall, our positions had been cut, and we would be returning to the classroom.

I was devastated. I had put everything into jumping into this exciting job, and it had blown up in my face. My position at East Tech had already been filled, so I couldn't return to that position. I had given away a ton of my stuff and would essentially be starting over without classroom supplies. Now, I had no idea where I was going to be in the fall. We were all assured that we would have jobs, as there were openings in all areas across the district; it just may not be our number one choice of positions. We were given instructions to refer to the transfer list for the district, email the director of human resources our top three choices, and HR would do their best to place in one of our choices.

I had put everything into jumping into this exciting job and it had blown up in my face.

I looked at the list later that night and started narrowing down some choices, but I wasn't in any hurry to email human resources. Part of me thought that perhaps it was a bad dream and that I would wake up from it and still have my digital learning coach position. However, when I woke up the next day for my last day at East Tech, I was disappointed to realize that I technically did not have a job after the end of the day.

Luckily, the first exam period of the day was my prep period, so I didn't have to face students and expose them to my disappointment. I cleaned up some things around my classroom and sat down at my computer to look at the list a little bit more. When I opened my email to access the list, I saw a message marked as urgent with the subject line of "CALL ME ASAP." The message was from Lucas Leavitt, my friend whom I met at the Google Summit previously that got me into presenting and really helped me discover my passion for technology and professional development.

I called his office, and he told me that he had heard what had happened with the digital learning coaches. We exchanged a few choice words about how we felt about the situation, but how ultimately there wasn't anything that I could do about. He turned the conversation to if I had submitted my list of positions to human resources, which I hadn't done at that point. He told me not to do anything and that he had a few calls to make and to hang tight. I told him I would wait on him and tried to get him to tell me what he was doing, but he said just to be patient and that he'd call me back.

It didn't take long for Lucas to get back to me. When he did, he told me that he had the principal of one of the high schools in the district on the line with us and that he wanted to talk to me. The principal on the line was Travis Warnick of Shadow Ridge High School. Mr. Warnick proceeded to tell me that he had a full-time digital learning coach at his school that had just left for another job and that since I was out of a job and he had an opening, he wanted to speak to me further, asking if I would be able to meet with him later in the day. After my last final, I got permission to leave school and meet with Mr. Warnick, and after a 20-minute conversation, I completed paperwork to submit to human resources to serve as a learning strategist over technology at Shadow Ridge.

In a span of fewer than 24 hours, I went from having a job as a digital learning coach working at a handful of schools, to not having a job at all, to having to peruse a list of openings in my district, to having a digital learning coach position at one school. It was a whirlwind that even when I think about it today, it stresses me out. Regardless of where I would have ended up, I would have made the best of it. But I was certainly happy with the result.

While I had spent several of the previous summers going to conferences, reading books, and planning for the following fall, I couldn't wait to jump into my new position. I had a ton of ideas that I wanted to try out to get to know my new colleagues, how to help them to earn my trust, and I really started to dive into different ways to use a variety of different tools. I even met with Lucas and Mr. Warnick for lunch one day to discuss some of my ideas, learning that I had 100% support from Mr. Warnick and my new supervisor, Mr. Ron Kamman.

But even though I was excited and expressed my enthusiasm with my new colleagues once the year began, that enthusiasm wasn't reciprocated by most of the staff. The more I tried to share and to help, the less of an impact I felt that I was making with staff. In the first month or so, I felt like it was because I was the new guy and that I hadn't earned their trust. But as time went on, the struggle continued. I was helping the same four to five people regularly. Some teachers flat out refused my help. Periodic emails that I sent to the staff with tech tips were, for the most part, unread. And rather than helping teachers with implementing various tools into their lessons, it seemed as if I was called upon to reset passwords and troubleshoot Chromebook and printers if I was called upon at all. I began to spend more and more time in my office creating presentations than I was in classrooms.

After a few months, I began to question my decision to pursue the digital coaching job. Regret isn't the right word, but I really began to think about how I could still be in the classroom, working with students, teaching history as I had done for the previous 11 years. While there was nothing I could do to take back that decision, I did have a couple of other options: stick with my job as a learning strategist working with teachers, and maybe things would improve or start looking at administrative positions that were open in the district.

There was no shortage of positions available when I started looking prior to winter break in 2016. When a position opened up, I would do some research about the school and make some calls to some friends around the district to see if they had any insight

After a few months, I began to question my decision to pursue the digital coaching job.

into the school. I looked at elementary assistant principal openings and middle and high school dean of students openings. If I applied, I put together a folder of various items that I would take to the school to hand-deliver to the principal, allowing me to introduce myself and inform them that I was looking forward to meeting with them about the position.

While the entire administrative team at Shadow Ridge was helpful in my pursuit of an administrative position, one of the assistant principals, Aaron Olson, was especially helpful. Mr. Olson helped me put together my folders, gave me suggestions of items to put in the folders, and took the time to conduct mock interviews with me in preparation for interviews with principals and their teams. Mr. Olson urged me to print my resume on high-quality paper rather than standard printer paper, provide a business card with my folder (I had some made specifically for my folders), and instructed me to put information about the school in which I was applying in my letter of interest. All of these things seem obvious to me now, but without Mr. Olson, I most likely would not have been called for the interviews that I was fortunate enough to get over the course of several weeks.

In the closing weeks of 2016 and into the first few weeks of 2017, I applied for seven different positions at various schools, and I received interviews at five of them. In the case of two schools, I received notification that I was not selected without further explanation. Tina Statucki, my old supervisor at East Tech, was principal at a third school, and she called me to tell me that she wanted to go with somebody with more experience, as it was halfway through the school year, and evaluations were due. With the other two schools, Chaparral High School and Thurman White Middle School, I made it to the top three, meaning further interviews.

The last interview in the process was with an area superintendent who oversaw the school in which you were a finalist. This interview was more of a conversation to get to know you rather than an interview. There wasn't a series of questions; it was definitely more casual than the previous interviews. After participating in two such interviews, it was now a waiting game to hear if I would be appointed or not.

If you have ever watched the movie, *The Pursuit of Happyness* (2006), you may remember the film's main character, played by Will Smith, saying, "If You Want Something, Go Get It. Period!" While I don't remember the movie well, as it has been a long time since I have seen it, I did stumble upon this quote reading a blog post by Paul Lous Heil III titled "If You Want Something, Go Get It. Period" - What It Really Means. In this post, Mr. Heil interprets this quote to mean that one must take action, be persistent, and expect nothing but give everything in order to get what you want in life.

Up to this point in my career, I embodied Mr. Heil's interpretation. I took risks and was persistent in my pursuit of my first teaching job, moving on from that first job to resurrect my career, discovering a passion for technology and professional development, pursuing my education further to become a leader, and even though there was a minor setback, obtaining a position as a technology coach. The same goes for my pursuit of an administrative position. For several months, I didn't sit back and wait for something to happen. I went out and put in the work to get it. And now, I was a finalist for two positions.

Which brings us back to the telephone ringing in my office at Shadow Ridge and Mr. Warnick calling me down to his office. All of those risks and hard work had paid off, and I was officially accepting a position as dean of students at Thurman White Academy of the Performing Arts. I thanked Mr. Warnick for his support over the past few months, went back to my office, called my wife and parents, and proceeded to pack up my office. Two days later, in a brand new shirt and tie, I walked up to Thurman White with a box of pictures and office supplies, stepped into the office and introduced myself to the office manager, who led me to my office where I would start the next step of my career as a school administrator.

Throughout your career, most likely, you have been compelled to move on from your position and try something new. After 11 years of teaching, I was compelled to challenge myself as a technology coach. After a short stint as a coach, I wanted to challenge myself as a school administrator. And I am a firm believer that the day that I no longer want to be challenged is the day that I need to retire or find another profession. If you are reading this, I am going to take a shot in the dark and assume that you are a person who loves a great challenge as well. And since you are up for a challenge, don't let any potential negative consequences get in the way of taking a risk to meet a challenge head-on.

Will there be growing pains? Absolutely! Will you have moments where you wish you had stayed put? Yep, sure will! But think about your growth as an educator and as a person. Will you be able to make the same strides if you stay put? Maybe, maybe not. When thinking about a new challenge, and contemplating the risk, consider the following questions:

- When you have wanted to move on and try something new, what has been the main reason for that desire? Boredom? Toxic school culture? Something else? Why do you feel this way?
- You acted on your desire to pursue a new challenge: GREAT! Whether it was teaching a new grade level, a new subject, administration, or something else, what did you do to maximize your chances to earn that new position or challenge?
- If you could go back in time, what would you tell your younger, less experienced self in regards to taking a risk and trying something new?

Share your story and your thoughts on Twitter using #ToTheEdgeEDU!

7. STRUGGLES

Whatsoever I've feared has come to life
Whatsoever I've fought off became my life
Just when every day seemed to greet me with a
smile
Sunspots have faded and now I'm doing time
Now I'm doing time
'Cause I fell on black days
I fell on black days

— *FELL ON BLACK DAYS BY SOUNDGARDEN*

The screen flickered, taking down the image of my face and fading to black. A split second later, Christie's face appeared. With her usual happy demeanor and a smile, she asked me how I was doing and how my week had been, to which I stated that it had been pretty good. With a no-nonsense tone, Christie asked me to remind her of where we had left off in our conversation previously. I thought about it for a second, reviewed quickly what I last remembered, and for the next hour, we chatted about a whole host of topics.

Christie was my therapist. Sessions with Christie were not like what you see on TV. For one, the sessions were via video chat, so the whole "lie on the couch while I jot stuff down in a notebook and ask a bunch of questions" was not how they were conducted. Another difference: Christie made it seem like a conversation between two people, not a doctor interviewing a patient. Her style made me feel like she truly cared about my well-being. But why was I talking to Christie in the first place? Why was I "going to therapy?"

If you were to describe me as a child, a teenager, a young adult, and even into the early years of my teaching career, depressed is not a word that would fit the profile. In fact, I was anything but depressed. Even during the awkward years of junior high where I got picked on quite a bit, it didn't bother me to the point where I was depressed. Sure, things would upset me and I would be sad at times, but mostly, if I wasn't happy, I was angry, but even that was infrequent. But all of that would change on January 14, 2010.

Throughout my life, my brother, Cody, was never very far away from me. He and I shared a bedroom growing up. We were three years apart, far enough apart to where we had our own friends, but close enough to where we did most everything together. We were typical brothers: we joked, we fought, we had each other's backs. The day my family dropped me off for college, I remember Cody, tears streaming down his face, telling me how much he was going to miss me. (I'm getting a little teary-eyed thinking about that moment as I write this.) But it was only four-and-a-half hours back home, so we would see each other often enough, and at this time, the Internet had started to take off, so things like AOL Instant Messenger were available for us to chat regularly.

Fast forward to the fall of 2003. I was going into my fourth year of school, and my brother, graduating the previous spring, was moving to Marquette to join me at Northern Michigan University, not only as a student but as a member of the football team as well. I am not ashamed to admit that he was an even better athlete than I. Everything that he did, his 40-yard dash speed, his vertical jump, his broad jump, pullups, everything except overall strength (i.e., bench press) was better than mine. He was a wide receiver and would be joining the team as a redshirt, much like I had done three seasons prior.

The problem was that Cody was not interested in school. While he was very smart, he struggled to get up in the morning and had no desire to go to classes. To put it lightly, he certainly indulged in the college life that gets a lot of first-year students in trouble. No matter what I did to try to motivate him, the college life just wasn't for Cody, and after failing out after the first semester, he stayed in Marquette and worked at Applebee's (just like I did, see, I told you we did everything together!).

Fast forward to the fall of 2004. I am going to school part-time, working full time, substitute teaching occasionally, and spending time with Mary. Cody's car broke down, so he was relying on me, his girl-friend, and his friends a lot to get around. One day after class, I came home to relax before going to work, and Cody said, "Kyle, can you take me to the Army recruiter's office?" Surprised, I asked him where that came from, as I had never heard him mention the Army or any interest in the military. On the way to the recruiter's office, he explained to me that he had screwed up school and that if he didn't do something, he was going to end up doing something even dumber. He asked me to go into the office with him for support, which I gladly obliged.

We met with the Army recruiter for a few minutes, with Cody doing most of the talking and me as a silent observer. Eventually, I had to go to work, but Cody said that he would have someone pick him up because he had more questions. Before I left, I told him not to sign anything because he needed to think about it, and while he was an adult, he owed it to our parents to let them know that he was considering the Army.

A couple of days later, Cody returned to the recruiter's office and signed the official paperwork to enlist in the United States Army. He learned that he would be going to Fort Benning in Columbus, Georgia, for basic training and that he would be leaving a few weeks later. He basically had enough time to get his personal items together, put in two weeks' notice at work, and head home to visit friends and relatives before leaving. While I was sad to see him go, I knew it was what he wanted, and it was probably what was best for him at the time.

Cody was an exemplary soldier. He was assigned to the 101st Airborne Division based at Fort Richardson, Alaska. He served a 15-month tour of Iraq from 2006-2007 before transferring to the 10th Mountain Division at Fort Drum, New York. With the 10th Mountain, he served a 12-month tour of Afghanistan from 208-2009, where he earned a Purple Heart for injuries sustained in an attack by Taliban insurgents. In all of these months that my brother was deployed, it was always in the back of my mind that the worst could happen, but it wasn't something I worried about constantly. Regardless, when Cody returned home in December 2009, my family and I were all relieved that he was home and that he would not be deployed again for a while.

Once Cody was home, we talked all the time. He would call me three or more times a week. We would text each other every day. We even played a game where we would send the lyrics to a song, usually a metal song, and if our lyrics stumped the other, that person owed the other a beer the next time we saw each other. For the record, we were really good, we didn't stump each other very often (or maybe that means we weren't very good...).

Cody called me on a Wednesday night, January 13, 2010. We talked for a while about life in general and how embarrassing it was that the Detroit Red Wings got beat 6-0 by the New York Islanders. Cody said that he was going to play hockey later that night, so he let me go so he could take a nap for a bit before going to play. I told him to have fun and that I would talk to him the next day.

It was midterms week at school. On that particular day, I had a midterm to give in the morning, a ten-minute break, then another midterm before students were dismissed for the day. During my break, I was milling about, chatting with students, when my wife, Mary, walked into my classroom. Immediately, I knew something was wrong, especially when she was crying. I asked her, "What's wrong?"

"Cody's dead! Cody's dead!" she wailed.

I couldn't say anything. I had just talked to him 15 hours prior. This had to be some sort of sick joke. But as she sobbed and hugged me, I knew that it wasn't a joke. Like a zombie, I walked next door into my friend Alison's classroom. She knew something was wrong and when she asked me, all I could say, rather nonchalantly, was that my brother was dead. She sprinted out of the room and returned a minute later with one of the assistant principals, who took Mary and me to his office. I could barely see the buttons on the phone through my tears as I dialed my parents' phone number. I fell apart when I heard my dad on the other end of the line, sobbing uncontrollably, confirming that Cody had been found dead in his apartment that morning after he didn't report for duty on the Army base.

My assistant principal told me to go home and do whatever I needed to do and not to worry about the remaining midterms or report card grades. On my way out, I stopped in the principal's office to tell them what had happened, stating that I was flying back to the Midwest to be with my family and that I didn't know when I would return. The principal's reply to me was not "I'm sorry" or "What can I do for you?" It was, and I'm paraphrasing, "Make sure your grades are done, and if you take more than five days, any day after that is non-paid." Still in a state of shock, I walked out and went home, but to this day, I still remember that heartless response from that principal.

Once home, Mary and I packed bags and bought one-way flights into Chicago, as my parents were living near Chicago at the time. The flights weren't until a few hours later, so I told Mary that I needed to go back to school and get my grades done, but before we could leave, there was a knock at the door. I opened the door to two Army officers, one of which was a chaplain. Both men expressed their condolences for our loss and informed me that any travel expenses would be covered by the Army and that if there was anything else that they could do, I could contact them at any time. I went back to school, finished my grades, then headed to the airport for what was sure to be a long flight.

When we bought our flights, we arranged for it to be the same flight that my sister would be taking from Reno to Las Vegas, then to Chicago. When we boarded the plane, we were three of fewer than 15 on the flight. The flight attendants were very friendly but could tell something was wrong. We explained why we were on the flight and the drink cart was promptly brought to us. For the next four hours, we each had several drinks and didn't pay for any of them. My dad and my Uncle Rick, who had driven to Chicago with my Aunt Mary from Detroit, picked us up at the airport and thus began the agonizing next few days of planning a funeral.

WHILE I CERTAINLY REMEMBER SADNESS FROM that time, I also remember seeing how many people cared about Cody. His funeral was held in our hometown of Alpena. Family and friends came to Alpena from all over the country. Several of my brother's fellow soldiers drove overnight from upstate New York for the funeral. Countless others sent cards and flowers. A friend of Cody's from high school even arranged for my family and me to attend a Detroit Red Wings game a few days after the funeral and put an "In Memoriam" message on the jumbotron during the first intermission. Eventually, I went back to Las Vegas, but the sorrow would take its toll for the next several months.

I didn't know what to do. The closest I ever experienced to that kind of sadness was when my grandmother passed, but she had been sick for a long time; Cody's death was so sudden and unexpected. To make matters worse, we learned from his autopsy that he had died from pneumonia, choking on fluid in his lungs in his sleep. I turned to eating, and worse, to drinking. I was already miserable in my job, and Cody's death only added to it, so I was going home and drinking almost nightly for several months.

After a few months, I stopped drinking as much, but I had gained a lot of weight from unhealthy eating combined with my drinking. I knew I had to do something about my weight, so I joined Weight Watchers. Within a year, I had lost nearly 70 pounds and was back to a healthier weight. But even though my brother's death was nearly two years prior, I still was constantly sad, and even little things like hearing a specific song would send me into a fit of rage, tears, or both.

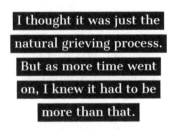

At first, I thought it was just the natural grieving process. But as more time went on, I knew it had to be more than that. But here's the problem: I wasn't willing to admit I was having trouble. I wasn't drinking heavily again, I wasn't abusing drugs, I wasn't overeating regularly. In fact, I was probably in the best shape of my life because I was training for half marathons and lifting weights, as well as playing rec league hockey. But my wife and I were arguing more, little things would anger me to the point where I would overreact, and I would "shut down" for hours, even days, on end where I would barely speak to anybody and hole myself up in my room.

This continued off and on for a long time. While I blamed my emotions on Cody's death, for the most part, it got to the point where I couldn't explain why I would wake up feeling down or shut down for days at a time. Between the negative stigma surrounding mental illness and the fact that I believed that I had a pretty good life with a family, friends, etc., it was just going to be something that I would need to cope with.

Finally, after several years of this kind of behavior, my wife gave me an ultimatum: get help or bad things were going to happen. It was at this point that I told her that I needed help and that I couldn't explain why I felt depressed and had long bouts of withdrawal from her, my family, and my friends. But what was I supposed to do? I have never been a person who has been an open book emotionally; I've tended to bottle up issues, many times until it is too late.

ONE OF THE most interesting books that I have read in recent memory is *The Subtle Art of Not Giving a F*ck* by Mark Manson. The premise of his book is to give one guidance in placing priorities on what one should care about, evaluating one's morals and values, and living a good life by caring for oneself and putting energy into things that matter. Manson also talks about how emotions are "feedback mechanisms" to let you know that something is going well or something is not going well, with the purpose of "nudging you" in the direction of making a positive change.

After reading this book, it seemed so obvious to me. Why couldn't I have taken these signals years ago and made a change? How different would my emotional well-being be had I been able to realize it? Again, it wasn't that I didn't recognize something was wrong; it was that I wasn't willing to admit it for a multitude of reasons.

The first step was to make it known that I was struggling and that I needed help. I decided to get everything out in a blog post. On March 4, 2017, I published a post on andersonedtech.net titled, "Highs & Lows." In it, I highlighted my struggles with depression and emphasized that I wasn't looking for sympathy, but if my story could help one other person to seek help, then my words had meaning. The reaction to my post was overwhelmingly positive, with several people asking if they could share my story and several others even sharing with me their struggles with depression.

Next, I sought out the help of a therapist. While writing my blog post, publishing it, and interacting with others about my post was hard, this was even harder for me to do. I was going to be revealing everything about myself to a complete stranger, one that would prod at me to reveal even more, and in my previous assumptions, possibly judge me for my behavior and emotions. But I knew I had to do it, so I made an appointment and nervously sat down on that couch for the first time to open myself up.

The first step was to make it known that I was struggling and that I needed help. Opening up was actually a lot easier than I thought. However, in any doctor/patient relationship, there needs to be a sense of connection, of trust. After a few sessions with this particular therapist, I didn't feel like I had that connection. In all of my sessions, I would sit down, my therapist would ask a quick question, then it seemed like I did all of the talking. I felt like I was talking to myself most of the time. Don't get me wrong, talking about the things that had been bothering me for a long time was starting to make me feel a little bit better. But I didn't feel like I was learning more about my issues; I was simply identifying the issues.

After a few weeks, I decided to move on from this particular therapist. I didn't know exactly what I wanted in a therapist, but I knew I needed something different. Chris Hardwick, the host of the ID10T Podcast (formerly the Nerdist Podcast), talks about therapy often on his show with his guests. He has talked in many episodes about how, while he has had the same therapist for many years now, it took him several sessions with several different therapists before settling on his current doctor. He has also likened his therapy to exercise: if you don't like a particular form of exercise, why would you force yourself to keep doing it? Continuing to see a therapist that you aren't gelling with is very similar, in his opinion.

Which brings me back to Christie. After my initial few sessions, I had a hard time finding somebody, for many reasons. For starters, finding a therapist was hard because most were completely booked and weren't accepting new patients. If I happened to find one that had openings, my research and quick conversations over the phone didn't give me confidence that they would be a good fit. Finally, I came across Christie, a former teacher that left education to become a therapist. She had previously worked in my school district and specialized in depression. She seemed like the perfect fit for me.

After a few minutes of getting to know each other in our first session, I felt like I had known Christie for years. I was very comfortable in answering any question she threw at me. But I didn't feel like I was being interviewed; it felt more like two people just trying to know as much about each other as possible. And because of her comfortable manner, we were able to come to a lot of realizations in my sessions.

Obviously, the pain of losing my brother had a lot to do with it. Because I had always tended to bottle things up (I only cried twice between learning of his death and the funeral, and I didn't cry at the funeral), we determined that I never had properly grieved and my way of coping was to mask my grief through bottling it up and turning to food and alcohol. But there were some other issues that we talked about that I would have never come up with on my own that, in hindsight, make perfect sense.

Shortly after moving to Nevada, my parents made a similar move. My dad took a job working for a company in Quincy, California, about an hour and a half from Reno, Nevada, and about nine hours from Las Vegas. While it was still a long drive, my parents were a lot closer than the three-day drive back to Michigan. A couple of years later, they moved again, this time to a small town about 45 minutes south of Chicago, Beecher, Illinois. It was Beecher where my parents lived when Cody passed away, and while we all met there in the days after his death, we made our way back to our hometown of Alpena for his funeral and where he is buried next to my grandmother.

When my parents left Alpena in 2006, I was still in school and wasn't able to go help them pack the house and move. They brought along a few boxes of my stuff that I had left there when I moved to Nevada, but the last time I was ever in the house that I grew up in was in the summer of 2005, a few weeks before moving to Nevada.

Christie theorized that the roots of my depression came before my brother's death and that it was two-fold: the separation from everything that I had known in my life and the lack of closure with my childhood home after my parents moved away. When she presented this to me, I laughed it off initially. But then I got thinking about it more. When I have dreams from which I wake and I have feelings of extreme happiness, oftentimes, they involve my hometown and my childhood home. My best memories involve the loft-like room at the top of the stairs, the enormous yard we had where we played sports, ripped around on our bikes, played hide-and-seek, and the woods and the pond connected to our property.

I am most likely never going to set foot in my childhood home again. However, at Christie's suggestion, when I start to feel down, I pull up a satellite image on Google Maps, zoom in, and it brings back a flood of great memories, especially when I see how big the trees in the yard are now compared to when I was a kid. And while I haven't done it in years, it was really nice to drive by my old house when I was back home visiting family and friends.

BECAUSE OF CHRISTIE and the risk that I took to admit my weakness and seek out help, I am in a much better place today. I still have struggles and have periods of shutting down, but they are less frequent, and the amount of time can be measured in minutes to hours, not hours to days as in the past. I can cope more effectively and do not resort to unhealthy mechanisms like drinking when I am feeling down. And while I still could be more open with people and share my thoughts, I have been better about getting my emotions out rather than bottling them up.

Like I wrote in that blog post back in 2017, this part of my story is not a ploy to gain anybody's sympathy. Depression and other forms of mental illness have reached epidemic levels in our world today. Millions of people struggle with mental illness daily, and some, unfortunately, turn to suicide as the only way out to ease their pain and suffering. Social media and cable news will point out the struggles of celebrities like Kate Spade, Robin Williams, Anthony Bourdain, Chester Bennington, and Chris Cornell after their tragic endings, but it's not just about celebrities; it's about all people, regardless of background, economic status, age, ethnicity, etc.

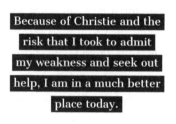

Because of Christie and the risk that I took to admit my weakness and seek out help, I am in a much better place today.

First and foremost, if you are struggling, seek help! There are tons of people out there that care for you and will drop everything to help you. I know from experience, and I feel closer to those people today than I ever had before. Talk to a loved one or friend, seek out counseling, or if it is immediate, call the Suicide Prevention Lifeline at 1-800-273-8255 (in the United States) or visit their website at www.suicidepreventionlifeline.org.

Be on the lookout for others who are struggling. Check in with people, ask them how they are doing, make it be known that you care about them. If you see a change in behavior, it's better to be wrong in your assumptions rather than to believe that everything is fine when it is not. As teachers, this is especially important, as so many of our students come from broken homes, are bullied, and have their own stories that may be contributing to depression and/or suicidal thoughts. Build relationships with your students and show them that you care about them. If you suspect that students are struggling, work with your colleagues to get students the help that they may need.

And lastly, the stigma surrounding depression, suicide, and other mental illnesses is real. But if people aren't more open about it, that stigma is not going to go away. In fact, after I wrote my initial blog post in 2017, I received a private message from somebody in my professional learning network (PLN) that gave me credit for opening myself up but advised against sharing the story too much as it may harm my career. But that cannot be a hindrance to opening up and seeking the help that you need. Your mental health is the number one priority, regardless of what others may think.

Mental illness has an impact on each of us daily in our personal lives and in our lives as educators. Consider the following questions:

- When you are feeling stressed or depressed, what are some things that you do to bring yourself back into a better state of mind?
- What do you do in your classroom or school to ensure a safe learning environment for students to share their emotions and improve their mental and emotional well-being?
- Celebrity struggles with mental illness and suicide are highly publicized when they happen, but then tend to fade away quickly. How can we continue the conversation about mental illness regularly without needing to rely on the up and down, 24-hour news cycle?

Share your story and your thoughts on Twitter using #ToTheEdgeEDU!

8. SWIMMING IN THE DEEP END

Until we try how will we know?
How will we know until we try?
So let's say we give it a go
To find the world that we're looking for

— *WOULDN'T IT BE NICE? BY PENNYWISE*

The radio crackled, startling me from the report that I was writing. The day had been a long one, one where I had barely gotten up from my desk. It was nearing the end of the school year, and spring fever was in full effect. It seemed as though the door to the dean's office had been a revolving door of referrals. One after another, students were sent to the office for various infractions, some of which were a simple call home, some of which were more severe, requiring more extensive disciplinary action. The voice on the radio was a welcome break from the monotony of report writing.

"I need assistance immediately!" said the voice coming from the radio, the voice of one of the campus security monitors. "I have a student destroying a classroom, I need assistance now!"

I sprang up from my desk and headed toward the door of the office. Right behind me was Josh, one of the other deans. Without assuming anything, we had a good idea as to what was going on and who the student might be. We had been to this classroom many times over the previous months. Often times, the calls that came to us embellished what was happening in the classroom, but if assistance was requested, we were on our way to provide it.

The scene we walked into was not embellished at all. The classroom was a disaster. Desks were overturned. Papers and books were strewn everywhere. A small group of students cowered in the corner while the teacher and the campus security monitor tried to calm the student who had been responsible for the mess. Upon seeing Josh and me, this student became more agitated, storming past us and out into the hallway.

The hallway didn't make matters better. Anything that could be torn from the wall or kicked aside was. A garbage can was thrown. A rack with rolls of colored paper was toppled over. The sound of screams brought students and teachers heads out of classrooms to see what the commotion was all about. Slowly, we were able to guide the student out into the quad. Our school police officer was waiting and was able to restrain the student.

This was the last that I ever saw of this student. As the incident was winding down, I thought about the destruction that had been caused over the past few minutes. I thought of the number of students whose education had been interrupted and, in some cases, who had been in physical danger as this student conducted their rampage. And I also thought about this: what was I doing here, and did I really want this to be what I did on a daily basis?

What was I doing here and did I really want this to be what I did on a daily basis?

I started my first day as a dean of students on a Friday in late February

2017. This Friday also happened to be a spirit day, with a school-wide assembly scheduled for the entire student body at the end of the school day with basketball games after school. This was most certainly not going to be a typical day as a school administrator. On top of that, outside of dropping off my folder to the principal and two interviews that were held at the school, this was the first time I had stepped foot in the school and didn't know a soul.

My principal arrived shortly after I did. She led me to my office so I could drop off my box of things, then began the rounds of introductions. Office by office, she stopped to introduce me to counselors, receptionists, the school nurse, registrar, and a host of others. I was also introduced to Josh Wikler. While we made our rounds, students began to arrive, decked out in their school spirit best. Before long, buses arrived, and the campus began to fill up, so we headed out to the quad for morning supervision.

It was at this point when it really began to set in what I was doing. The principal introduced me to students and gave me some pointers and expectations for supervision duty. She also explained to me that I would be shadowing Josh for the first week or so until I got acclimated to the rigors of the job. Between all of this, teachers were coming up to introduce themselves and what they taught. It was quite overwhelming, to say the least!

Throughout that day and over the next week or so, I began to pick up on what needed to be done. I spoke to students who had been referred to the office. I learned the intricacies of the discipline management system and how to complete the referrals that were sent. I met with the teachers that I would be evaluating, using a few of my own observations and observation notes that had been completed by the previous dean. Josh and our other dean, April Barr, were very helpful in my transition, and for the most part, I felt like I was settling in nicely.

The work was demanding, for sure. There was rarely a moment of calm, and scheduling a time to eat was nonexistent. From the moment I walked in each morning to the time I left in the afternoon (or evening on many days), it was a nonstop grind of seeing students, meeting with the administrative team, observing teachers in action, morning, lunch, and passing period supervision, and much more. When it came time for sleep, I had no trouble whatsoever.

When I was appointed, there were about three months left in the school year. My perception was that it would be a good amount of time to learn the position, write some evaluations, and go into the summer with a few weeks off to prepare for a full year as an administrator and school leader. The hours were long, the stress level was high, but I chalked that up to being new and that the next school year would be better.

AFTER A FEW WEEKS, I went back to start the 2017-2018 school year at the beginning of August. I had about two weeks before students started back, but I had a ton of things to take care of before that. The other deans and I had to prepare a presentation for students for our dean's orientation. I had bussing maps and schedules to prepare so students knew where to go to catch their bus each day. I had teacher observation forms to prepare so I could effectively observe and evaluate teacher practice. The responsibilities seemed endless, but I was assured that once school started, things would start to calm down some, and I would be able to get into a routine.

The first day of school approached, and I was overwhelmed. It seemed that whenever I got one thing done, four more things would pile up on top of the other things that I still had to do. My days were even longer than when there were students at school. I was going into school in the morning around 7:00 and not leaving until well after 7:00 that evening. And I was taking work home, something that I hadn't done probably since my first year of teaching. (I have told myself that I would rather stay at school a little longer to get things done rather than take it home, that time is for my family and me.) And even though I was asking for help, I was making mistakes one after another, having to spend even more time on tasks, adding more to the stress of things that I had to get done.

However, my biggest mistake was yet to come. With the help of the dean's office manager, I created posters with bus route numbers, where they would pick students up each day, and maps of the school to help students find their busses. Tired after a long week, I looked at the pile of posters in the dean's office and decided that I would take care of them first thing on Monday morning prior to students arriving for the first day of school. I locked up my office and headed home for a weekend of rest before what would be a crazy week.

When I walked in early on Monday morning, the posters were nowhere to be found. After searching for what seemed like hours, I tracked down one of the custodians, dreading the worst. The custodian confirmed my fear, stating that the posters had been thrown away, mistaken for a pile of garbage. Now I had to scramble to come up with something to help students to find their way to their buses after school. The quick solution was to print sheets with each bus route's information and give each student a copy as they got off of their bus. The posters could be taken care of throughout the day.

My principal was not happy. Shortly after students reported for their first class, she asked me to come to her office, where she expressed her disappointment in my mistake. I left that meeting feeling like a failure. Had I simply taken the extra time on Friday to hang the posters, all of this would have been prevented. Unfortunately, this would not be the end of my mistakes, ranging from forgetting to complete simple tasks, setting up the auto dialer to notify parents of school announcements, and misjudgments on discipline assigned to various students' infractions.

I was questioning if I wanted to continue in administration. I kept telling myself that it would get better, I just needed to grind my way through, but it wasn't getting better. I was spending 12-14 hours a day at school, I was taking work home, so I was barely seeing my family and not spending any time for myself. My principal was frequently frustrated with my work. I wasn't sleeping well and woke up many mornings sick to my stomach and dreading going into school.

The straw that broke the camel's back came about a month and a half into the school year. My principal emailed me one afternoon, instructing me to meet in her office the next day at 9:00. I knew that it couldn't be good; usually, she would put meeting information in the email when she sent it or would tell me to stop by when I could. The next morning, I walked in to see the principal and the assistant principal and was asked to close the door, confirming my fear that this wasn't going to be a good meeting.

My principal proceeded to tell me that she didn't think I was making any improvements in my performance. She listed off a series of things that I had done (or not done) that she felt were not good enough. She gave me the opportunity to explain why I was

> I kept telling myself that it would get better, I just needed to grind my way through, but it wasn't getting better.

struggling, to which I didn't have an answer other than that there wasn't any excuse. She asked again, so I opened up. I explained that I was completely overwhelmed, I never got to see my family, I wasn't sleeping, and I felt that I was walking on eggshells with everything that I did, afraid I was going to mess up on just about everything that I did. I am not a crier, but tears started to stream down my face as I explained that I didn't know what to do at that point.

What she said next devastated me. Essentially, my principal told me that I showed a lot of promise in my interviews and brought a lot of great skills to the position, but that at this point, my hiring had been a disappointment. Through my tear-filled eyes, I looked up, wondering if she had really just said that. Realizing that my ears hadn't played tricks on me, I choked out the following: "I can't do this anymore, I want to go back to the classroom." My principal nodded and told me that she would make some calls and make my request happen as quickly as possible.

This moment still haunts me today. I had truly quit a job for the first time in my life. My first job working as a dishwasher and cook in high school? I left for college and couldn't work there anymore. My job as a custodian in the dorms? I moved out of the dorms, and you were required to live there to work as a custodian. My job at Applebee's? I moved to Las Vegas after graduating from college. Sure, I had switched schools a couple of times prior, but I never felt like I had ever really quit a job. Even now, some people will tell me that all I had to do was stick it out and it would have gotten better, but there were so many reasons why I made the request to go back to the classroom.

The time and the stress, no doubt, was most of the reason why I was not happy as a dean. But many other things contributed to it as well. As a dean, my chief responsibility was student discipline. Positive student interactions were rare in my office. When a student came to my office, it was because they had been referred to me for various infractions. My interactions, as much as I tried to be positive, were discussing with them the reason why they were sent to me, why they need to learn from what they did, and the discipline assigned, such as detention or in-school suspension. The negative interactions really took a toll on me, and I knew that if I went back to the classroom, I could have more control over student interactions and make them more positive.

Not every interaction was negative. Supervision duty was a time of joking around with kids, asking about their basketball and soccer games, chatting music with the kids wearing punk and metal t-shirts, and checking in with kids who had been in my office for negative reasons. However, the days were filled with tardy referrals, instances of insubordination, breaking up occasional fights, investigating bullying claims, or protecting students from the student who had destroyed a classroom and the hallway before the police escorted him away. It was hard to stay positive with that as the constant.

WHEN I DECIDED I wanted to be a school leader, I wanted to be a leader so I could have an impact on students by helping teachers. I wanted to be that administrator that was rarely in my office because I was in classrooms, observing teachers, providing feedback, perhaps even modeling or co-teaching a short lesson occasionally. While I know that I should have prioritized this, I wasn't able to get into classrooms as much as I wanted to. By the time I got done taking care of student discipline business, the school day had ended, and teachers and students had gone home. My biggest regret from my short time in administration is not being more of a leader in the classroom, and, instead, spending more time in my office.

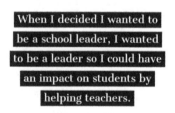

I had never worked with middle school students before, outside of student teaching. I have always worked with high school students. Middle school students are a lot different than high school students in many ways, especially emotionally. Because of my inexperience with working with middle school students, I struggled. Things I could say to a high school student that elicits a quick yes or no response may cause tears or a profanity-laden tirade from a middle school student.

And lastly, while disappointment and failure are a part of life, I don't like to be labeled as such, as nobody does. Once I heard those words from my principal, even if I misunderstood what she meant by it, that was a dagger. Had I continued on, it would have made it that much harder for me, in my opinion, knowing that I was already struggling and that I had to earn back a reputation that I was not a disappointment. I respect that principal still, I most certainly deserve the criticism that I received, but the biggest take away from that moment, and the moment where my principal neglected me in the moments after learning of my brother's death, is perfectly aligned with a quote that is often attributed to Maya Angelou: "I've learned that people will forget what you said, people will forget what you did, but people will never forget how you made them feel." (A quick Google search shows millions of results that give Angelou credit, but still others from reputable sources that state that she did not say this.)

I have not dismissed returning to administration one day. Perhaps it was just not a good time with a young family. Perhaps it wasn't the right school and the right team to work with. Perhaps I need to gain more experience in leadership in another fashion first before diving into the deep end of the pool again. Regardless, I don't regret my time as an administrator, and it has helped me tremendously in many areas since returning to the classroom, especially in student-teacher relationships, defusing difficult situations with students, families, and colleagues, and it has given me an appreciation for the amount of time that administrators put in to make a school work.

After my meeting where I requested to go back to the classroom, I felt a wave of relief wash over me. While I didn't know where I would be going or how long it would take, I knew that I had made the right decision and would soon be returning to the classroom, albeit nearly two months into the school year. My principal also gave me permission to use a personal day or two over the next couple of days while the process of transferring panned out. I was expecting at least a couple of weeks before I would hear something, so in the meantime, I headed back to my office to do my job, something that as long as I was there, I was going to continue to do.

Much to my surprise, I got a phone call a couple of hours later. My request had been approved, and I was emailed a list of schools with openings in which I was qualified to teach. The list was very short, only two schools, and both positions were physical education, a subject that I minored in during college and was licensed to teach but had never done so in my career. One school was a standard high school, the other an alternative behavioral school where students were sent after removal from school for disciplinary reasons. I was instructed to get back to my principal as soon as possible with my decision as to where I wanted to go.

I am always up for a challenge. Teaching physical education for the first time was certainly going to be a challenge. The standard high school was in an upper-middle-class neighborhood but would have class sizes of 60 or more students. The alternative school would have much smaller class sizes, but would have students with disciplinary issues that more than likely came from tough neighborhoods, families, etc. Ultimately, because I wanted to have an opportunity to be more positive with students, I chose to go to the alternative school. I believed that if anybody needed a positive influence in their life, it would be the students who had made mistakes and were sent to an alternative school. I notified my principal, and she told me that she would pass along my decision to human resources and that I would be starting the following Monday, less than a week after I made my initial request.

In my short time as an administrator, I felt that I made some great connections with a few of the teachers at the school. The day before my last day, I stopped into one of the social studies teacher's classrooms to tell him the news. He was on his prep period, and I ended up chatting with him for about 45 minutes. He told me that he was in the same boat at one time: taught for several years, became a dean, and left it shortly after appointment to go back to the classroom. His reasoning was very similar, and he expressed his support for my decision, even though he did assure me that I would be missed by many at the school.

Later that day, we had a staff meeting in the school library. The meeting had been planned from the beginning of the year as one of the monthly meetings. At this one, however, I would be announcing my decision to move on from the school. So after a few minutes of standard business, my principal informed the staff that I had an announcement. I swallowed hard and stood in front of nearly 100 educators to tell them that the next day would be my last day. A collective gasp went through the room with looks of utter surprise on many faces. As the meeting adjourned, most of the staff came to me to thank me for my time and to wish me good luck. I left that day feeling like I still made the right decision, but felt that I had been appreciated for the work that I did in my short time there.

In her book *Be REAL*, Tara Martin talks a lot about how to "cannonball in." What she means by this is to take risks by not waiting for the perfect time. Rather than simply dipping your toes in the water, jump in, tuck your legs and your head, and make as big of a splash as you can. Was it the perfect time for me to become an administrator? Absolutely not! There is never going to be a perfect time for one to do anything, so why cannonball in and see what happens? And while you are contemplating how you can make a splash in your next risk, consider the following:

- We all have times where we feel overwhelmed as educators. Think about a time where you felt so overwhelmed that you didn't think you could keep your head above water and wanted to get out of the pool. What did you do to make the situation better?
- What have you always wanted to do as an educator or as a person but have not because you are waiting for the perfect time?
- People say hurtful things, even when they sometimes mean well by their words. As an educator, think of a time that

somebody that you respected said something to you that was devastating. What did you learn from that incident, and how has it made you a better educator?

Share your story and your thoughts on Twitter using #ToTheEdgeEDU!

9. DOING WHAT'S BEST

Oh, life is waiting for you
It's all messed up, but we're alive
Oh, life is waiting for you
It's all messed up, but we'll survive

— LIFE BY OUR LADY PEACE

The sun beat down from the sky through the haze of smoke from several wildfires across the region, reflecting off of the truck and the nearby buildings. Kevin, wiping sweat from his forehead, reached for a beer and groaned, "Man, it is HOT today!" Chuckling, I said, "It ain't that bad, it's only in the mid-90s! It was like 115 when I loaded this truck the other day!" It was definitely hot, but after living in the Mojave Desert of Southern Nevada for 13 years, the mid-90s was a nice reprieve from the usually late July temperatures that barely and rarely dipped below 100, even in the nighttime hours.

"Only a few more things, and this truck is empty. Let's suck it up and get it done, then we can enjoy the rest of the day," chimed in Quinton.

Kevin and Quinton had graciously given up part of their Saturday to help me unload a 27-foot U-Haul truck. Some of the stuff had been unloaded the night before and brought into my new apartment, while the rest of it was getting unloaded into a storage unit a few miles away. Some furniture, a few boxes of books, some fishing gear and my bag of hockey equipment disappeared behind the sliding metal door of the unit, a padlock secured the door shut, and it was off to return the moving truck and unpack boxes in the comfort of air conditioning.

The kids were a few hours away at my parents' house near Redding, California. The new apartment that Mary and I were setting up was in Reno, Nevada. We were settling into our apartment and making a home out of it. Boxes and packing materials lay everywhere, but slowly but surely, the apartment began to look livable. But after so many years in Las Vegas, why was I unpacking boxes at a place in Reno?

For several years, my wife, Mary, had been working as a speech pathologist in the school district in Las Vegas. At one point, she earned a master's in early childhood education, but she wanted more. She wanted her master's in speech so she could expand her skillset and opportunities in her field. A bachelor's degree in speech could only get her work in the school districts in Nevada; every other state and private practice require a master's degree. But regardless of the schools to which she applied, she had not been accepted to a program.

After coming home one day from my new position as a physical educa- tion teacher, Mary and I had a discussion about the future and her wishes to continue her education. The schools from which she was rejected had all been online programs, so she asked if I would be willing to move somewhere so she could pursue a more traditional master's program. To me, this was a no brainer: I would absolutely go wherever necessary for her to further her education.

Over the years, I had completed two degrees online. I experimented with different roles in education, as a teacher, a technology coach, an administrator, and now a PE teacher. But Mary had stayed in one place as a speech pathologist, and while not complacent in her work, she really wanted to go back to school but could not gain acceptance into a school. To make matters worse, Southern Nevada did not have a graduate program in speech pathology. So moving somewhere was going to be the only option we had for her to fulfill her dream.

After careful consideration, Mary narrowed down her choices of schools to three: Western Michigan University, Grand Valley State University (Michigan), and the University of Nevada, Reno. She spent several weeks throughout the fall of 2017 preparing everything she needed for her applications, and we researched the job and housing markets for each area. We both knew that the process was going to take a while, so once she submitted the applications, we entered into a game of "hurry up and wait."

IN THE MEANTIME, I was enjoying my new role as a PE teacher, for the most part. The days were much shorter, I wasn't bringing any work home, I was active outside nearly all day, every day, and I was on the phone contacting parents a lot less than I had been in my previous position as a dean. Days could be very tough; after all, my students were those with behavioral issues, and with that, many students had issues with authority figures, common courtesy, and appropriate language that most educators take for granted in their classroom. Simple requests to put away PE equipment could be met with a profanity-laced tirade. Many students were gang members, and rival members would often taunt one another and even resort to physical fighting at times. But overall, 80% of my days were very good, 20% not so good, which is about par for the course at every school in which I have worked.

After a few months, the constant redirection for inappropriate behavior, language, and more started to get old. The negativity was taking its toll on me mentally. I started seeing my therapist once a week if only to voice my frustrations of work. My coworkers and principal at the school were very supportive, as they were experiencing the same thing. But while some students were very tough, there were many more who were trying to learn from their mistakes and do their best to minimize their time in the school so they could go back to a regular middle or high school. Still, I found myself counting down the days to the end of the school year, but unsure of what the next year was going to bring me.

What saved me during this trying period was the words of Todd Nesloney and Adam Welcome in their book, *Kids Deserve It!* Mr. Nesloney and Mr. Welcome talk extensively about doubt in their book and how doubt can make one question if they are having an effect on students, their families, colleagues, etc. I was most definitely having doubts. Was I really having a positive impact on my students, or was I simply just another adult in their life that could potentially let them down?

> I found myself counting down the days to the end of the school year, but unsure of what the next year was going to bring me.

Reading this book during this time made me realize that even though there were going to be tough kids that were going to be defiant and seem unappreciative, there were plenty of students that were positively affected by my presence. Even the tough students, deep down, needed me as well, even if they didn't show it on the outside. So many of my students came from homes where they were abused, physically and emotionally, and had to grow up a lot faster than they should have. Many of my students were taking care of siblings or finding jobs to help support their families. Parents were in prison, dead, or had abandoned them. Very few of my students had a trusting adult in their lives, and their way of coping was to lash out and behave in a manner that isn't considered proper. But Nesloney and Welcome reassured me that I was doing right for my students, regardless of my doubts. Still, it wasn't going to be easy, especially with the uncertainty of the future and not knowing where my family and I would be in a few months.

MARY WAS STILL WAITING to hear back from schools as the calendar turned to 2018. I had made up my mind that if Mary did not get into grad school, I wanted to go back to a social studies classroom, so the chances of remaining at the alternative school were not very high. But Mary and I both were banking on her acceptance to school somewhere, so I continued to check job boards on availability for houses and apartments.

Her answers would come in late February and early March. She would receive acceptances from Grand Valley State and Nevada. With the great news, though, came tough conversations and evaluations: where would we go, and what factors would help to determine where we would go? There were so many things to discuss. Moving expenses, cost of living, availability of jobs for me (Mary wouldn't be working, school would be too time-consuming), salary and benefits, and if there was any support network of family and/or friends that we could rely on were all a big part of the discussion.

There were pros and cons of each location. For Grand Valley, we would be moving back to Michigan, the state where Mary and I both grew up. We both had lots of friends that lived in the area that could give us pointers on where to live and be a friendly face in a new place. My hometown was about 4 hours away, so seeing my grandpa and uncles would be a lot easier. But job opportunities were very few and far between, even when expanding my radius of commute to over an hour, and because I would be coming from out of state, most districts would not honor my years of experience, resulting in a massive pay cut, making it even tougher to support a family.

A move to Reno so Mary could attend the University of Nevada made more sense. We had traveled to Reno frequently to visit my parents, who live about three hours from Reno in Northern California, so seeing my parents more often was a possibility. We liked the city and the surrounding area, and I knew a handful of people from the connections that I had made on Twitter. While fewer districts than Southwest Michigan, there were more job openings for me, and my years of experience would be fully considered since I was coming from a district in Nevada. I would also continue to contribute to the retirement system in Nevada rather than sacrifice the 13 years I had accumulated.

After careful consideration, Mary decided to enroll in the program at the University of Nevada. I was so incredibly happy for her, as she had worked so hard for so long to get to this point. We knew that there was certainly going to be sacrifice and that it wasn't going to be easy, but ultimately, it would be for two years, and the sacrifices made would be totally worth it. So now that we knew where we were going, I had to get a job so I could support the family.

What I began to find was that jobs weren't as plentiful as I first thought. The openings I had discovered weren't available to outside applicants, only to in-district transfers. I was going to need to expand my radius to find a position in something in which I was licensed to teach. But even then, pickings were slim. However, I was assured upon applying for the applicant pool of the Washoe County School District in Reno that positions would start opening in the late spring. However, late spring was too late for my anxiety; I wanted to be assured of a job sooner than that knowing that I could support my family.

At this point, a representative of WCSD asked me if I was willing to teach special education. Based on my teaching license, I could teach secondary social studies, physical education, and health, and I could serve in administration. However, the representative from human resources said that they didn't anticipate many openings in any of these areas, and in order to work in administration, I had to work in the district for at least a year first. If I was willing to complete some classes to become licensed in special education, the district would give me up to three years to complete the requirements while I worked as a special education teacher. At this point, I was willing to do anything to support my family.

In surrounding districts, the story was much of the same. Openings in my licensed areas of instruction were simply not available. I did apply for a district-wide technology coaching position in a nearby district but was notified a week after submission that the position had been filled. Districts over the border in California had a few openings, but the requirements of obtaining a California teaching license, a salary cut, and the thought of having to commute through feet upon feet of snow in the winter put those applications on the back burner as a last resort; I needed to stay in Nevada if I could. Then I remembered a conversation I had at an anniversary party for Tina and Craig Statucki a few months prior.

In August 2018, Tina and Craig celebrated their 25th anniversary at their home with dozens of friends and family. At this point, Mary had been considering applying to school and had compiled a shortlist of schools. Tina introduced me to her sister, Tasha, at the party. Tasha served as the principal of Carson High School in Carson City, a 30-minute drive south of Reno. Previously, she had been an administrator in Reno and knew a lot of other administrators around the district. She urged me to contact her if we made a move to Northern Nevada as she would do what she could to help me in the process of finding a job.

I drafted an email to Tasha, telling her the good news that we were moving to Reno and that I would like to take her up on her previous offer. She replied that she would be more than happy to help and suggested I look around the Carson City School District for positions. While Carson High didn't have any social studies positions open, the district would also consider me for special education if I completed the coursework required to become licensed, much like Washoe County. Carson High had an opening in special education, so I decided to apply. In addition, I applied for several special education positions at various schools in Reno, hoping to hear back from somebody with an offer of an interview.

———

IT WAS NOW late May and the school year was nearly finished. I'm not going to lie, knowing that I was leaving, I was checked out. Going to work each day became more of a struggle, but I kept telling myself that it was almost done and that a new beginning was close. The stress of not knowing what I was doing was starting to build, but I had applications out on several schools, so something was bound to happen.

About a week before school let out, I received an email from Carson High School asking to schedule an interview for their special education opening. They asked if I would be able to do a video conference and to be prepared with a short lesson to demonstrate during the interview. I was excited and relieved! Finally, a potential job! However, on the day of the interview, I received an email asking to reschedule as one of the people on the interview panel was unavailable. Since school was ending and I would be off the following week, I asked if I could schedule an in-person interview, to which I was informed that I could. So now, I had about a week to prepare for the interview and the lesson that I would be presenting during the interview.

Once school was out, it didn't quite hit me that my time at the only school district in which I worked was over. Over the course of 13 years, I had made a lot of great friends and memories and had impacted thousands of students. But there wasn't time to celebrate as I had to focus on getting my next job. So we packed up the car with about a week's worth of clothes and headed to Reno where we would look for a place to live, enroll my daughter, Elsa, in school for the following fall and find a preschool for my son, Reed, and then head to my parents' place in California to relax for a few days.

I woke up at about 4:30 on the morning of my interview. My interview wasn't until 8:00, but I couldn't sleep any longer. This was going to be the most important interview that I had in a very long time. Previous interviews, while important, were for positions that I wanted. This was for a position that I wanted but, more importantly, a position that I needed. I took my time getting ready, stopped at Starbucks to get a coffee, and made the half-hour drive out to Carson City.

I was led to a conference room where three individuals were waiting, smiling, and introducing themselves

This was going to be the most important interview that I had in a very long time.

as I entered the room. I was asked a series of questions about my experience and skills, which I was able to answer confidently. When questions were presented about my skills in teaching special education, I wasn't as confident. While I had co-taught in my career and worked with students with special needs regularly, I wasn't familiar with all of the ins and outs of teaching special education. I answered the questions to the best of my ability and hoped that the panel liked what they heard.

Any fear of not answering questions effectively was dashed once I presented my lesson. I had prepared a short lesson on Japanese internment during World War II using Pear Deck. Nobody on the panel had ever seen Pear Deck before and was dazzled! In addition to asking questions about my lesson, they asked several questions about Pear Deck, which then led to a discussion on my knowledge and skills with educational technology. What was initially an interview of about 20 minutes turned into a lively conversation of about 45 minutes.

After the interview, I got back in my car and headed back to Reno, informed that somebody would be getting back to me regarding the position. I was confident that I had done well and felt relieved, especially because Tasha had not been on the panel. I feared that she was going to be a part of the interview panel, and I feared that my previous work with her sister, Tina, could have potentially compromised my interview, especially if the others on the panel knew of our connection. Whether they knew before the interview or not, I don't know. Either way, it didn't matter, because about 45 minutes later, my phone rang.

I didn't recognize the number, only the area code, 775, the area code of the State of Nevada outside of Las Vegas and Clark County. My first thought was that it was a school from Reno looking to interview me for an opening. But then my thoughts turned to, "Is it Carson High? Have they made their decision already?" I pressed the phone button on the steering wheel and answered, "Hello, this is Kyle!" The voice on the other end was familiar, as it was the assistant principal of Carson High School that had been part of the interview panel less than an hour prior. She proceeded to tell me that they were very impressed with my experience, my skill set, and my overall display of confidence and was curious if I would like to come work at Carson High School? Ecstatic, I excitedly accepted her offer and asked about the next steps.

I got back to the hotel room a few minutes later to find Mary and the kids getting ready. We had a few things to do around Reno, then a three-hour drive to California to get to my parents' house. I tried to keep as straight of a face as possible. Mary asked, "Well, how was your interview?" I smiled and said, "It went well enough that they called me a few minutes ago and offered me the job!" Mary and Elsa sprinted across the room and mobbed me while Reed, only three, sat on the floor, wondering what the commotion was all about. The pieces were falling into place.

A couple of months later, we packed up our belongings, said goodbye to our friends, and watched the City of Las Vegas disappear in the rearview mirror. Our new apartment was only about a third of the size of our previous home, but it is what we could afford on one salary. Much of our stuff wasn't going to fit in the apartment, hence the storage unit that Kevin and Quinton helped me fill.

While transitioning to a new city, a new school and district, and making new friends has not been easy, it has been an amazing journey thus far, and after watching me pursue my dreams for years, Mary deserves to do the same, so the sacrifices we have made have been totally worth it. Consider the following questions:

- What sacrifices have you made in your life and career to pursue your dreams? Do you have any regrets, or would you have done something differently in hindsight? Why or why not?
- Think about something that you want to do in your career in

the future. What is it going to take to achieve that goal? What sacrifices will you need to make?

- Making sacrifices takes a strong support network? Who do you turn to for support in these situations?

Share your story and your thoughts on Twitter using #ToThe-EdgeEDU!

10. WHAT ARE YOU WAITING FOR?

No, you don't know what you will give up
You don't know what you want
It may take you years to find out
You don't know what you need
It's something that may never come to you

— Disconnected by Face to Face

The road before me appeared to climb forever, at least until it disappeared around a curve to the north. With 15 miles already behind me, my legs were screaming at me from guiding the bike over the rolling hills. But the hill in front of me seemed insurmountable after what I had already done. I clicked the triggers on each end of the handlebars to get the bike down to the lowest gear, stood up on the pedals, and started the grind of nearly two miles and a gain of nearly 1,000 feet.

Sweat was pouring off of me, even though it was a pleasant 75 degrees, and the sun was disappearing behind the mountains. Traffic was light, so the sound of silence surrounded me as I struggled up the hill. I kept telling myself that as soon as I got to the top, my lungs would get a reprieve with a three-mile downgrade. My pace was slow, to the point where I could probably walk more quickly, but I was determined to get to the top of the hill without stopping.

As I turned the corner, I could see the summit. While it was only about a half of a mile away, with the way my legs were burning, it may as well have been 20. But I could see the end in sight, and there wasn't anything that was going to stop me at that point!

As I approached the summit, I noticed something in my peripherals in the late evening twilight. In the distance, an opening in the hills to my right revealed the lights of downtown Reno that had begun to show against the silhouette of the mountains northeast of the city. I stopped at the top of the mountain to marvel at the beauty and solitude around me. I couldn't believe that I lived in a place so beautiful. I was maybe five miles from the hustle and bustle of a small city in the high desert, but from my vantage point, it felt like I was across the world. At that moment, I realized how lucky I was to have had the strength and confidence to do so many of the things that I had in my life. With a deep breath, I swung my leg back over the bike, sat down, and began pedaling, clicking the bike into higher gears, preparing for the downslope before me.

Risk-taking is scary at times. You don't know what the results of your risks are going to be. Risks can have a multitude of consequences, some great, some horrific. But while one must evaluate the consequences of risks, the potential negatives shouldn't scare one into not taking a risk.

Throughout this book, I have highlighted numerous instances in my life where I took a risk to better myself as a person and as an educator. In many instances, the risks I took produced rewards beyond comprehension. But in others, the risks I took did not produce the results that I had hoped for. But while I may have had regrets in the immediate aftermath of a risk that did not pan out, I can confidently look back now without regret, knowing that the risks that I have taken have made me the person that I am today.

A COMMON STORY that has been passed along for years claims that Michael Jordan was cut from his basketball team as a high school sophomore. Jordan could have easily given up, but he decided to put in the work to improve his game and take the risk to try out for the team again the following year. The rest is history, as Michael Jordan is regarded as one of the greatest basketball players of all time.

While most of us will not become the next Michael Jordan, think about where your risks may take you if you are willing to put yourself out there. Had I not taken the risk to leave home and head off to college four hours away, who knows where I would be. Had I not finished up my degree and moved across the country with a woman that I had known for less than a year, who knows where I would be. Had I given up on myself as an educator and moved on to something else, who knows where I would be. If I hadn't gone to that first Google Summit or agreed to present to my peers, would I have discovered my passion for educational technology and learning with my peers and PLN? There are so many questions that beg answers that cannot be provided.

Today, I am the happiest in my career that I have ever been. I have enjoyed transitioning to special education, completed a master's degree in special education (I like to joke now that I am one of the most educated people in the school without a doctorate, as I now have two master's and an educational specialist degree), and I get to work with teachers sharing my passion and knowledge of educational technology. I try to post to my blog a couple of times a month, and I am the co-host of two podcasts, The BeerEDU Podcast with Ben Dickson where we chat about two things we love, education and beer, and The Podcast by

Sons of Technology with Joe Marquez where we encourage people to embrace change in education, challenge the status quo, and try new things with technology.

There are many moments in your life and career where you will be brought to the edge, wondering what the next step should be. When standing on the edge, look to potentially great things that will happen. Don't completely disregard the negatives; they must be taken into account. A skier when ready to conquer a double black diamond run doesn't think about losing an edge, tumbling down the mountain and breaking a leg; the skier thinks about the exhilaration of conquering a tough run with numerous obstacles and the sense of accomplishment when making it to the bottom. As an educator and as a person, I want to embrace that sense of risk-taking in my everyday life.

While in the process of finishing my draft of this book, I was talking to John Eick, executive director of Westlake Charter School in Sacramento, California. We were discussing the premise of this book and the message I was trying to convey in writing it. John, the epitome of optimism, stated that he couldn't be more excited that I was telling this story. His reasoning: he thought that the concept of taking a risk was something that was fading somewhat in our current world, especially in the younger generation. He felt that too many people "play it safe" and don't put themselves out there to achieve what they want, instead settling for the status quo and for comfort. In his words, he wishes that people would "tear it up and make some bad decisions" more often for the sake of learning opportunities and that some people may regret not taking more risks later on in their life.

In the vein of John's words, I hope that my story has been an inspiration to you in some way, shape, or form. I hope that it has inspired you to try some things that perhaps you wouldn't have done before, whether it is a new tool in your classroom, pursuing an advanced degree, or making a cross-country move to take that dream job that you may have never thought of doing. And I hope that it has also inspired you to model risk-taking with your family, friends, and colleagues, inspiring them to be better people by taking themselves to the edge and embracing risk in their lives.

When I started my blog years ago, I closed out my first post with three words that stuck with me and has been the closing line in every post I have had since. I believe it is appropriate to do the same here, so I will leave you with that.

Until next time...

ACKNOWLEDGMENTS

Thank you for being a friend
Traveled down a road and back again
Your heart is true, you're a pal and a confidant

— THEME SONG TO THE GOLDEN GIRLS

This book would not have been possible without several people in my life. There is no way possible that I can thank everybody that has had an impact on me and inspired me to tell my story. Just know that even though I may not mention you, you know who you are, and I thank you for your friendship and inspiration over all of these years.

First of all, thank you to my parents, Marshall and Lori Anderson. I have been a total and complete pain in your neck for a long time, but thank you for raising me to be the confident man that I am today. My sister, Brandi, I apologize for scaring off every boy that tried to talk to you when we were younger, so thank you for sticking with me in the pursuit of my dreams. And Cody, while you are no longer with us physically, your memory and spirit live on in so many things, and you are a continued inspiration to me through the hard work and determination that you displayed in your short time on the Earth.

My extended family of my grandpa, my aunts, uncles, and cousins, while we don't see each other as often as we'd like, know that I miss you each day and think about you often and your support over the years.

My brother from another mother, Brandon Genwright, what can I say? There aren't words to describe what you mean to me and the things that we went through together. I am proud to be an uncle to your children, and thank you for bringing my sister from another mister, Lorrin, into my life. Our terrible impressions of old Jerky Boys sketches and movie quotes will never get old. I look forward to the day we are sitting in rocking chairs on the porch as old men reminiscing about days gone by.

To my friends of over 20 years, where would I be without you? Andy Kelsch, Adam Ferris, Ryan Baker, Nic Wiser, John VanDusen ("JVD"), Angie Corthals (Indish), Ellie Crow (Walker), Amy Krause (Ayotte) (you introduced me to Mary!), Vern Harlock, Brian Scarbrough, Mark Brewer, Ashlee Peterson (DeDuijtsche), Ryan DeDuijtsche, Kristen Boyer, and so many more!

To those that helped guide me and mentor me to become the educator that I am today, Jayme Rawson, Rickee Moss, Alison Levy, Tina Statucki, Carrie Boehlecke, Craig Statucki, Glenda Goetting, Josh Wikler, Heidi Carr, Lucas Leavitt, Travis Warnick, Ron Kamman, and many, many more! Thank you for your guidance, your confidence in me, and the beers we have had together!

To my PLN, where do I begin? You are always there at any given moment for inspiration, suggestions, innovative ideas, and so many of you have become great friends IRL (in real life)! Jon Corippo, Adam Juarez, Kat Goyette, John Eick, Brian Briggs, Ryan O'Donnell, Tom Covington, Kristina Mattis, Kristina Allison, Laurie "EdTechYoda" Wong Roberts, Randall Sampson, Brent Coley, Coach Ben Cogswell, Ann Kozma, Eddie Campos, Tara Martin, both Matt Millers, Brent Warner, and so many more have pushed me to be a better educator and person, and I cannot thank you enough for being there for me!

To the teachers and coaches that I have had throughout my life, you shaped me into the educator and man that I am today! Mr. Stoll, Ms. Wallis, Mr. Romstadt, Ms. Clute, Mrs. Keskimaki, Ms. Wojt, Mr. Bell, Mr. Meek, Mr. Pintar, Coach Linton, Coach Gribble, Coach Collins, Coach Jurasin, Dr. Nicholson, Dr. Ferrarini, Mr. Poli, Mr. Caderette, and so many more! I hope that you read this and realize the impact that you have made on me!

Ben Dickson and Joe Marquez, thank you for being a part of an amazing journey with our podcasts, The BeerEDU Podcast and The Podcast by Sons of Technology. Getting to learn from and with you on a regular basis recording our shows is an absolute blast, and I look forward to years of episodes and continued learning!

To the team at EduMatch Publishing, thank you for taking a chance on me and letting me tell my story, I cannot thank you more!

Don't be afraid, take yourself to the edge and risk it!

And most importantly, to my wife, Mary. You have put up with me for a very long time, we have been through some crazy ups and downs, but I wouldn't have it any other way. You have given me two awesome kids, Elsa and Reed, and you have supported me in every crazy thing that I have wanted to do in my life. I don't know how I can ever repay you for that. I love you so much and look forward to growing old with you and all the other crazy stuff that we come up with!

And thank you, the reader, for taking the time to read my story. Without you, my story wouldn't mean a thing, and I hope that you have found some inspiration from my words to tell your own story and take more risks. Don't be afraid, take yourself to the edge and risk it!

NOTES

Introduction

Biazzi, Marco, et al. "Lacuna Coil – To the Edge." *Genius*, 31 Mar. 2006, genius.com/Lacuna-coil-to-the-edge-lyrics.

Maloney, Deirdre. *Tough Truths: The Ten Leadership Lessons We Don't Talk About*. Business Solutions Press, 2012.

Chapter 1

"SNL Transcripts: Christina Applegate: 05/08/93: Matt Foley: Motivational Speaker." *SNL Transcripts Tonight*, 3 Jan. 2019, snltranscripts.jt.org/92/92smattfoley.phtml.

Richmond, Tisha. *Make Learning Magical: Transform Your Teaching and Create Unforgettable Experiences in Your Classroom*. Dave Burgess Consulting, Incorporated, 2018.

Coley, Brent. *Stories of EduInfluence: 10 Life-Changing Powers to Unleash in Your School*. EduMatch Publishing, 2018.

Chapter 2

Staley, Karen. "Faith Hill – Let's Go to Vegas." *Genius*, 1 Jan. 1995, genius.com/Faith-hill-lets-go-to-vegas-lyrics.

Data Access and Dissemination Systems (DADS). (2019). *American FactFinder - Results. Factfinder.census.gov.* Retrieved 29 June 2019 https://factfinder.census.gov/faces/tableservices/jsf/pages/productview. xhtml?src=CF

Maloney, Deirdre. *Tough Truths: The Ten Leadership Lessons We Don't Talk About.* Business Solutions Press, 2012.

Chapter 3

Smith, Adrian. "Iron Maiden – Wasted Years." *Genius*, 6 Sept. 1986, genius.com/Iron-maiden-wasted-years-lyrics.

Wong, Harry K. *The First Days of School.* Harry K. Wong Publications, 1998.

"What We Do - Teach For America." *Teach For America.* 2019. Retrieved 29 June 2019, from https://www.teachforamerica.org/what-we-do

Chapter 4

Shanahan, James. "In Ashes They Shall Reap." *In Ashes They Shall Reap Lyrics*, 29 Sept. 2009, www.lyrics.com/lyric/17801846/In+Ashes+They+Shall+Reap.

Burgess, Dave. *Teach Like a Pirate: Increase Student Engagement, Boost Your Creativity, and Transform Your Life as an Educator.* Dave Burgess Consulting, Inc., 2012.

Casa-Todd, Jennifer. *Social LEADia: Moving Students from Digital Citizenship to Digital Leadership.* Dave Burgess Consulting, Inc., 2017.

Chapter 5

Incubus. "Incubus – Drive." *Genius*, 26 Oct. 1999, genius.com/In-cubus-drive-lyrics.

Couros, George. *The Innovator's Mindset: Empower Learning, Unleash Talent, and Lead a Culture of Creativity*. Dave Burgess Consulting, Inc., 2015.

Maloney, Deirdre. *Tough Truths: The Ten Leadership Lessons We Don't Talk About*. Business Solutions Press, 2012.

Chapter 6

Bowie, David. "David Bowie – Changes." *Genius*, 7 Jan. 1972, genius.com/David-bowie-changes-lyrics.

Heil, Paul Louis. "'If You Want Something, Go Get It. Period' - What That Really Means." LinkedIn, 1 Sept. 2014. Retrieved 14 July 2019, from www.linkedin.com/pulse/20140902062100-60388198--if-you-want-something-go-get-it-period-what-that-really-means/.

Casa-Todd, Jennifer. *Social LEADia: Moving Students from Digital Citizenship to Digital Leadership*. Dave Burgess Consulting, Inc., 2017.

Muccino, Gabriele, director. *The Pursuit of Happyness*. 2006.

Chapter 7

Cornell, Chris. "Soundgarden – Fell on Black Days." *Genius*, 8 Mar. 1994, genius.com/Soundgarden-fell-on-black-days-lyrics.

Manson, Mark. *The Subtle Art of Not Giving a F*ck: A Counterintu-itive Approach to Living a Good Life*. HarperLuxe, 2016.

Anderson, Kyle. "Highs & Lows." Anderson Edtech, 4 Mar. 2017.

Retrieved 14 July 2019, from www.andersonedtech.net/2017/03/highs-lows.html.

Chapter 8

Dragge, Fletcher, et al. "Pennywise – Wouldn't It Be Nice." *Wouldn't It Be Nice Lyrics*, 22 Oct. 1991, www.lyrics.com/lyric/2342434/Pennywise/Wouldn%27t+It+Be+Nice.

Martin, Tara. *Be REAL: Educate from the Heart*. Dave Burgess Consulting, Inc., 2018.

Chapter 9

Halligan, Dee Dee, and Junior Torello. "Life." *Life Lyrics*, 12 Dec. 2000, www.lyrics.com/lyric/4567898/Our+Lady+Peace/Life.

Nesloney, Todd & Welcome, Adam. *Kids Deserve It! Pushing Boundaries and Challenging Conventional Thinking*. Dave Burgess Consulting, Inc., 2016.

Chapter 10

Riddle, Mark, and Trevor Keith. "Face to Face – Disconnected." *Genius*, 26 Aug. 1993, genius.com/Face-to-face-disconnected-lyrics.

Gold, Andrew M. "Thank You for Being a Friend (Theme from 'Golden Girls')." *Thank You for Being a Friend (Theme from "Golden Girls")* *Lyrics*, www.lyrics.com/lyric/12104144/Andrew+Gold/Thank+You+for+Being+a+Friend+%28Theme+from+%22Golden+Girls%22%29.

OTHER EDUMATCH TITLES

EduMatch Snapshot in Education (2016)
In this collaborative project, twenty educators located throughout the
United States share educational strategies that have worked well for
them, both with students and in their professional practice.

The #EduMatch Teacher's Recipe Guide
Editors: Tammy Neil & Sarah Thomas
Dive in as fourteen international educators share their recipes for success, both literally and metaphorically!

EduMatch Snapshot in Education (2017)
We're back! EduMatch proudly presents Snapshot in Education (2017).
In this two-volume collection, 32 educators and one student share their tips for the classroom and professional practice.

Journey to The "Y" in You by Dene Gainey
This book started as a series of separate writing pieces that were eventually woven together to form a fabric called The Y in You. The question is, "What's the 'why' in you?"

The Teacher's Journey by Brian Costello
Follow the Teacher's Journey with Brian as he weaves together the stories of seven incredible educators. Each step encourages educators at any level to reflect, grow, and connect.

The Fire Within
Compiled and edited by Mandy Froehlich
Adversity itself is not what defines us. It is how we react to that adversity and the choices we make that creates who we are and how we will persevere.

EduMagic by Sam Fecich
This book challenges the thought that "teaching" begins only after certification and college graduation. Instead, it describes how students in teacher preparation programs have value to offer their future colleagues, even as they are learning to be teachers!

Makers in Schools
Editors: Susan Brown & Barbara Liedahl
*The maker mindset sets the stage for the Fourth Industrial Revolution,
empowering educators to guide their students.*

Divergent EDU by Mandy Froehlich
*The concept of being innovative can be made to sound so simple. But
what if the development of the innovative thinking isn't the only
roadblock?*

EduMatch Snapshot in Education (2018)
EduMatch® is back for our third annual Snapshot in Education. Dive in as 21 educators share a snapshot of what they learned, what they did, and how they grew in 2018.

Daddy's Favorites by Elissa Joy
Illustrated by Dionne Victoria
Five-year-old Jill wants to be the center of everyone's world. But, her most favorite person in the world, without fail, is her Daddy. But Daddy has to be Daddy, and most times that means he has to be there when everyone needs him, especially when her brother Danny needs him.

Level Up Leadership by Brian Kulak
Gaming has captivated its players for generations and cemented itself as a fundamental part of our culture. In order to reach the end of the game, they all need to level up.

DigCit Kids edited by Marialice Curran & Curran Dee
This book is a compilation of stories, starting with our own mother and son story, and shares examples from both parents and educators on how they embed digital citizenship at home and in the classroom.

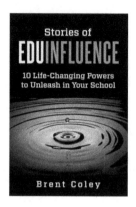

Stories of EduInfluence by Brent Coley
In Stories of EduInfluence, veteran educator Brent Coley shares stories from more than two decades in the classroom and front office.

The Edupreneur by Dr. Will
The Edupreneur is a 2019 documentary film that takes you on a journey into the successes and challenges of some of the most recognized names in K-12 education consulting.

In Other Words by Rachelle Dene Poth
In Other Words is a book full of inspirational and thought-provoking quotes that have pushed the author's thinking and inspired her.

To Whom it May Concern
Editors: Sarah-Jane Thomas, PhD & Nicol R. Howard, PhD
In To Whom it May Concern..., you will read a collaboration between two Master's in Education classes at two universities on opposite coasts of the United States.

One Drop of Kindness by Jeff Kubiak
This children's book, along with each of you, will change our world as we know it. It only takes One Drop of Kindness to fill a heart with love.

Differentiated Instruction in the Teaching Profession by Kristen
Koppers
Differentiated Instruction in the Teaching Profession is an innovative way to use critical thinking skills to create strategies to help all students succeed. This book is for educators of all levels who want to take the next step into differentiating their instruction.

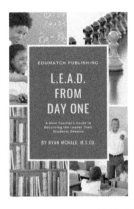

L.E.A.D. from Day One by Ryan McHale
L.E.A.D. from Day One is a go-to resource to help educators outline a future plan toward becoming a teacher leader. The purpose of this book is to help you see just how easily you can transform your entire mindset to become the leader your students need you to be.

Unlock Creativity by Jacie Maslyk
Every classroom is filled with creative potential. Unlock Creativity will help you discover opportunities that will make every student see themselves as a creative thinker.

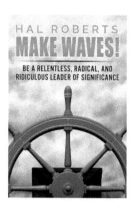

Make Waves! by Hal Roberts
In Make Waves! Hal discusses 15 attributes of a great leader. He
shares his varied experience as a teacher, leader, a player in the N.F.L.,
and a plethora of research to take you on a journey to emerge as
leader of significance.

21 Lessons of Tech Integration Coaching by Martine Brown
In 21 Lessons of Tech Integration Coaching, Martine Brown provides a
practical guide about how to use your skills to support and transform
schools.

Everyone Can Learn Math by Alice Aspinall
*How do you approach a math problem that challenges you? Do you
keep trying until you reach a solution? Or are you like Amy, who gets
frustrated easily and gives up?*

EduMagic Shine On by Sam Fecich, Katy Gibson, Hannah Sansom,
and Hannah Turk
*EduMagic: A Guide for New Teachers picks up where EduMagic: A
Guide for Preservice Teachers leaves off. Dr. Sam Fecich is back at the
coffee shop and is now joined by three former students-turned-friends.
She is excited to introduce you to these three young teachers: Katy
Gibson, Hannah Sansom, and Hannah Turk.*

Unconventional by Rachelle Dene Poth
Unconventional will empower educators to take risks, explore new ideas and emerging technologies, and bring amazing changes to classrooms. Dive in to transform student learning and thrive in edu!

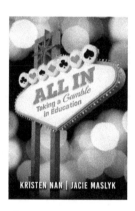

All In by Kristen Nan & Jacie Maslyk
Unlike Nevada's slogan of "what happens in Vegas, stays in Vegas," this book reminds us that what happens in the classroom, should never stay within the classroom!

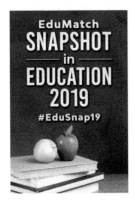

EduMatch Snapshot in Education 2019
EduMatch® is back for our fourth annual Snapshot in Education. Dive in as an international crew of educators share a snapshot of what they learned, what they did, and how they grew in 2019. Topics include Social Emotional Learning, identity, instructional tips, and much more!

Play? Yay! by BreAnn Fennell
Play? Yay! is a book my mom wrote for kids. I'm a toddler, and I like to read. I sit and look at pictures or point to my favorite pages. Do you like books like that? Then this book is for you too! The best part about this book is that you can read it with people like moms, dads, or grandparents. Get Play? Yay! today for fun, rhymes, and the gift of imagination.

The EdCorps Classroom by Chris Aviles
Something happens when you launch an EdCorps in your classroom.
An EdCorps, or Education Corporation, is what you get when you
teach your curriculum through entrepreneurship. In this how-to guide,
Chris Aviles tells you how he accidentally stumbled into the world of
student-run businesses, and how you can use them to provide authentic
learning to your students.

Strive by Robert Dunlop
This book will get you thinking about how happy you are in your
career and give you practical strategies to make changes that will truly
impact your happiness. Packed with research and inspiring stories, you
will end each chapter inspired and excited to try new job-embedded
ways to find more joy at work.

Thinking About Teaching by Casey Jakubowski
Teaching is by far one of the most intellectually rewarding, emotionally challenging, and physically exhausting careers in the world. This book explores the thoughts that author Casey T. Jakubowski, PhD has on a wide range of education related topics. Seeking to give voice to rural education, in this unstable time, and reflecting on a wide of research and experiences, this work offers all educators, from the beginning, all the way to the end, a reflective voice to channel their own experiences against and with on their journey.

I'm Sorry Story by Melody McAllister
Do you know what it's like to sit by yourself at lunch? Do you know how it feels when it seems everyone around you has close friends except you? That's exactly how Ryan feels. He wants good friends and he wants to be accepted by his classmates, but he isn't sure how to make that happen. Join him as he learns to put others first and make things right when he has been wrong!

EduMatch Publishing

ABOUT THE AUTHOR

Kyle Anderson is a passionate educator with experience in a variety of settings, including high school social studies, educational technology coaching, middle school administration, middle and high school physical education, and special education. Kyle also coached for many years, working with student-athletes on the football field, the baseball diamond, and the volleyball court. In addition, Kyle helped organize a ski & snowboard club at one of his schools, sharing his love of the mountains and snow with his students in the desert.

Besides taking risks and trying new things with his students and colleagues, Kyle is passionate about many things. Kyle enjoys attending and presenting at educational conferences and sharing his knowledge and passion through his blog, Anderson EdTech, and two podcasts, The BeerEDU Podcast and The Podcast by Sons of Technology. Kyle loves to travel, seeing the national parks and hidden gems all over the United States, and hopes to eventually visit every Major League Baseball park. Kyle loves to read, especially biographies and books on historical events. He loves watching hockey, baseball, and college football and basketball. As a former athlete, he loves to be outdoors, whether it is camping, hiking, fishing, or biking. And Kyle loves music, especially classic rock, hard rock, metal, punk, and ska.

Kyle and his wife, Mary, have two children, Elsa and Reed, and live in Reno, Nevada, surrounded by the splendor of the high desert, the snowcapped Sierra Nevada, and nearby Lake Tahoe.

Connect with Kyle!
Twitter: https://twitter.com/AndersonEdTech
LinkedIn: https://www.linkedin.com/in/andersonedtech/
Instagram: https://www.instagram.com/andersonedtech/
Blog: http://www.andersonedtech.net/
Email: andersonedtech@gmail.com